ULTIMATE MAKEOVER

Ultimate Makeover

THE TRANSFORMING POWER OF MOTHERHOOD

CARRIE GRESS

BEACON PUBLISHING

North Palm Beach, Florida

ISBN: 978-1-942611-71-4 (hardcover)
ISBN: 978-1-942611-72-1 (softcover)

Design by Jenny Miller

Excerpts first appeared in: CatholicVote.org: "Can We Have It All? Is the Wrong
Question," September 23, 2013; Catholic World Report: "A Brief History of
Same-Sex Marriage and Why Catholics Are Losing the War Against It," February
13, 2014; "Motherhood: The Ultimate Makeover," November 11, 2014.

Library of Congress Cataloging-in-Publication Data
Names: Gress, Carrie, author.
Title: Ultimate makeover : the transforming power of
motherhood / Carrie Gress.
Description: North Palm Beach, FL : Beacon Pub., 2016. |
Includes bibliographical references and index.
Identifiers: LCCN 2016015168 (print) | LCCN 2016016008 (ebook) | ISBN
9781942611714 (hardcover : alk. paper) | ISBN 9781942611721
(softcover : alk. paper) | ISBN 9781942611738 (ebook)
Subjects: LCSH: Motherhood--Religious aspects--Christianity.
Classification: LCC BV4529.18 .G754 2016 (print) | LCC
BV4529.18 (ebook) | DDC 248.8/431--dc23

For more information on this title or other books and CDs available through the
Dynamic Catholic Book Program, please visit www.DynamicCatholic.com.

The Dynamic Catholic Institute
5081 Olympic Blvd • Erlanger • Kentucky • 41018
Phone: 1–859–980–7900
Email: info@DynamicCatholic.com

Second printing, May 2018

Printed in the United States of America

*For my mother and my children,
with gratitude for your lessons,
large and small.*

Table of Contents

Foreword

From my experience as a mother, grandmother, and founder of Project Rachel, I have spent most of my adult life thinking about what it means to be a mother and the unique gift it is from God. There is nothing fiercer and more beautiful than the love a mother has for her child.

The women I have encountered who have experienced a pregnancy loss have been a stirring testament to just how profoundly the reality of biological motherhood is imprinted in our bodies. These women never met their children, and yet they mourn them, miss them, and suffer from loss no matter the circumstances. These women, rather than simply going along with their lives as they were before the healing process, often become the most outspoken voices for life and the gift of motherhood.

To engage in motherhood today is a radical choice, a choice not held in esteem by many. The fruits of motherhood, however, are powerful. I have seen again and again that motherhood moves us beyond ourselves. Each child teaches us something new about ourselves and helps us to grow from self-centered young women into wise and loving mothers. Many women I have spoken with are surprised by the virtues that have been honed through mothering, such as humility, courage, temperance, compassion, self-sacrifice, generosity, meekness, and patience. It is easy to miss these interior treasures in the day-to-day chaos.

Ultimate Makeover is an outside-the-box view of motherhood that offers a new perspective for not merely surviving but thriving as a mother today. It examines both the challenges of motherhood and the many hidden rewards it offers by looking at the vices and virtues that come naturally to women. The book looks carefully at how the *vocation* of motherhood is so much more than a *job;* it is rather a unique calling from God to go outside one's self. Both biological and spiritual motherhood call us to reach beyond ourselves to connect with and affirm others spiritually, psychologically, and humanly.

My own definition of motherhood is "women who are the practical responders to any situation." It is not limited to biological motherhood, but to any woman who is able to see the needs of others and respond in a way that is helpful, healing, affirming, and life-giving.

This book is an invitation to discover the wonder of motherhood—to realize that, as women, our call to nurture is a major gift from God and a large part of the *feminine genius* that Pope St. John Paul II spoke about in his 1995 letter to women.[1]

Pope Francis, who has spoken frequently of the important vocation of mothers, recently said:

> Mothers are an antidote to the spread of a certain self-centeredness, a decline in openness, generosity and

concern for others. In this sense, motherhood is more than childbearing: it is a life choice, entailing sacrifice, respect for life, and commitment to passing on those human and religious values which are essential for a healthy society. A society without mothers would be an inhuman society, because mothers are always able to witness, even in the worst moments, tenderness, dedication, moral strength.[2]

Motherhood is a special call from God to imitate Mary and her yes—her fiat—to love even when it hurts. It is not always wine and roses—far from it—but something more wonderful and important. Motherhood is the essential thread that weaves together the very fabric of our society.

Ultimate Makeover offers a whole new way to look at being a woman, illuminating the best we have to offer. Women have their own unique calling—a beautiful calling, as Edith Stein expresses so well:

> The soul of a woman must therefore be *expansive* and open to all human beings;
>
> it must be *quiet* so that no small flame will be extinguished by storm winds;
>
> *warm* so as not to benumb fragile buds;
>
> *clear*, so that no vermin will settle in dark corners and recesses;
>
> *self-contained*, so that no invasions from without can imperil the inner life;

empty of itself and also of its body, so that the entire person is readily at the disposal of every call.[3]

The following pages offer an examination of motherhood that is realistic and honest; Carrie Gress does not skirt the challenges and the hard times. More than a survival guide, this book shows how motherhood really is the ultimate makeover, transforming mothers into wise and radiant women who provide untold value to their families and society as a whole.

—Vicki Thorn, founder of Project Rachel

Ideas So Old
They Are New

Imagine you were offered a makeover that not only promised to make you more beautiful, but shaved off the rough edges of your personality and helped you gain control of your emotions, better manage your relationships, and grow in wisdom. And what if it could actually make you happy? Not waiting-for-happy. Not looking-in-all-the-wrong-places-happy. Not I've-given-up-on-happy. But truly, deeply happy—the kind of abiding happiness that isn't shaken by changes in fortune, life challenges, death of loved ones, or illness. Sounds too good to be true, huh? And yet, this is the makeover every woman is handed with the gift of motherhood. Oh, yes, you also get a darling little bundle, but the real rewards are just waiting to be claimed. I know, it sounds like an empty sales pitch, but bear with me.

Motherhood is hard. There is no way around it. I didn't realize just how hard until I started having my own children. It is the most difficult thing I've ever done—harder than learning four new languages, harder than writing a dissertation, harder than balancing full-time work and school. For a long time, however, I lived with the expectation that somehow being a mom was going to get easier. At every stage, I hoped that maybe next week I would get more sleep, that the endless messes would abate, or that the little battles through the mundane would subside.

A wise priest once told me that my daily struggles, such as being cut off in traffic, waiting in long lines, or dealing with incompetent customer service agents, were all part of God's plan to make me holy. A few days later, when my husband did something irritating, I looked at him with a clenched jaw and said, "You are making me so holy right now," which made both of us laugh. Somehow, however, I didn't apply this priest's wisdom to all the chaos and rough edges associated with parenting. Like most moms, I just wanted to get beyond them, rather than consider that maybe they were actually good for my soul and for our family in general.

And then the light finally went on. Being a mom is not going to get easier. The troubles and struggles may change, but various challenges will always remain. Why? *Because the crosses associated with motherhood are a feature and not a flaw.* Once I resigned myself to the reality that being a mom includes a healthy serving of struggle, a weight was lifted. Motherhood became *almost* easy once I accepted that it is hard. But the difficulty of motherhood is not in vain. This is an easy reality to forget when one is in the middle of what seems to be an endless slog. Motherhood, in fact, is the perfect antidote to the vices that come so readily to the fairer sex: vanity, impatience, pride, greed, unbridled emotions, over-controlling, and fickleness, to name a few. The daily struggles are God's way of making us over in his own image and likeness. The pains and frustrations are his way of saying, "Uh, you really need to work on this. . . . Oh, and maybe we could just put that vice here, out of the way. Yes, uh-huh. In the trash. . . . And how about if we move a bit more of this pretty stuff in?" He is the one who has given us life, the gift of a husband, and the blessing of children—and not just for us to remain the same person we were when we got married, but to transform us into saints.

A Spiritual Registry

The baby industry rakes in roughly $23 billion a year. Expectant mothers spend huge amounts of money and time preparing to bring their newborns home. Precious little time and thought, however, go into preparing a woman's soul for the most powerful, wonderful, natural, scary, overwhelming, and enduring experience of her life: motherhood. We may have all we need physically in preparation for baby's arrival, but are we prepared spiritually? Nowadays, most women don't give it much thought—one or two kids . . . how hard can it be? And yet from the earliest days of our education, most women are not exposed to the types of daily demands that a mother juggles. By and large we have been focused on some type of career outside the home, so when we find ourselves home with children we are bored, frustrated, overwhelmed, and ready to be "done." And yet, if you asked women, "Would you have more children if it weren't so hard?" most would say yes. I've encountered plenty of older women who say, "I wish I'd had more." It is because it is hard that most people resist the idea of doing it more than once or twice. But it is the hard part that is the best-kept secret. Among the daily trials are hidden doorways to the kind of motherhood we aspire to: joyful, wise, ordered, dignified, loving, and a whole host of other good things.

Feminine vices, however, can only be transformed into virtues through challenges. It's like building up muscles—no one expects to become a bodybuilder without lifting weights. Similarly, the virtues can't be attained without resistance. Motherhood offers opportunities to replace our vices with virtues, remaking us into the person God intends us to be.

It is only in this spiritual training that we can begin to see our lives, our pains, our struggles as fruitful. It's not just in the big things, like labor and childbirth, in which our pain has purpose and bears visible fruit—but in the everyday moments, like when you are so tired, you use your ATM pin to try to microwave soup. And yet, God in his great mercy has offered us this sanctification through the most gentle of ways: those little faces and grubby hands.

Feminism's Failures

Today, Western women who live with unprecedented wealth, health, and opportunity don't report being very happy. Despite the years of aggressive feminism promising the liberation of women through various government, social, and technical apparatuses, today, one in four women (29 percent) are on antidepressants, 11 percent are on antianxiety medication, eight million suffer from drug or alcohol addiction, and obesity rates have never been higher. In the thirst to find meaning and happiness, virtually no stone has been left unturned: New Age religions; yoga; divorce and non-traditional relationships (70 percent of divorces in the U.S. are initiated by women); fad diets; abortion (30 percent of females in the U.S. have had an abortion); and unprecedented personal debt all reflect the bottomless search. Even the dramatic rise in owning pets points to the unmet inner yearning created by feminism's failed promises.

Cultural pundit Camille Paglia, an outspoken feminist, has even noticed the problem: "Wherever I go to speak, whether it's Brazil or Italy or Norway, I find that upper-middle-class professional women are very unhappy."[4] She continues:

> Men and women never had that much to do with each other over history! There was the world of men and the world of women. Now we're working side-by-side in offices at the same job. Women want to leave at the end of the day and have a happy marriage at home, but then they put all this pressure on men because they expect them to be exactly like their female friends. If they feel restlessness or misery or malaise, they automatically blame it on men. Men are not doing enough; men aren't sharing enough. But it's not the fault of men that we have this crazy and rather neurotic system where women are now functioning like men in the workplace, with all its material rewards.[5]

Paglia makes it clear, even from her vantage point, that women trying to be just like men and expecting men to be just like women is a significant source of *un*happiness.

This unhappiness underlines the old adage that "nature always wins." *Humans are hardwired to be unhappy when they live outside of God's plan for their lives.* Imagine expecting a dog to act like a cat—even chemically altering Fido to be more like Felix. The image of a bulldog strutting around like a finicky feline would not make us think, "Oh, how free!" Instead, it just seems odd. And yet this is the subtle indoctrination women have adopted with wild abandon over the decades under the banners of freedom, choice, and equality, with little to no resistance.

Women are finally beginning to take notice that feminism's promises aren't filling that void in our hearts. After generations of rejecting the lifestyles of our great-grandmothers, their wisdom is coming back around. Although more slowly in secular culture, a renaissance of sorts is happening among Christian women. Many have committed themselves to being open to having more children than the national average (just under two); often they are educating their children at home; they have a strong commitment to their faith and deep desire to do God's will first, above all else. Surprisingly, many of these women have left the workforce, putting aside for a while high-paying jobs and careers as doctors, lawyers, corporate executives, and academics. These Christian women have found something much deeper to rely upon than trends and emotions: the will of God and the natural happy-making order he has set up on earth. At the heart of Christian motherhood is the clear understanding that God's ways are not our ways and that our enduring happiness can only be found in his ways. Only in the mind of God can one find happiness and daily struggle simultaneously reaching toward the same goal.

The Catholic Church has a long history of liberating women, despite what current popular culture might tell us. It may seem ironic, but Christianity has been the most liberating force for women in all of human history. Scripture going back to the Book of Genesis affirms the equality and complementarity of men and women—both are necessary to get a full, although dim, understanding of the nature of God. And while Judaism did much to honor the dignity of women, polygamy was something still considered appropriate, so a full appreciation of womanhood never blossomed. Christ's coming and his relationships with women changed the whole order of thinking about women. Rather than being viewed as second-class citizens, women were given their natural place of equality with men in sanctity and dignity (although of course there have been individuals who haven't lived out this reality and who won't in the future because of original sin). It is easy to look at the all-male priesthood and Church hierarchy and conclude that women have been mistreated by the Church. But the Church, in her wisdom, has said that men and women each have unique gifts—let's honor those instead of trying to pretend differences don't exist. Trying to turn women into men because men's actions appear to be more valued is no way to honor women.

Why This Book?

This book does not have the answers for every challenge and situation women face in motherhood. It doesn't offer tips on organizing your home or getting dinner on the table by six o'clock, but what it does offer is a new way of looking at your situation in light of God's unique call for your life. It goes to all those places in our souls that we would rather hide, while shedding light on how to change them. Although this book is written with mothers in mind, large sections of it will resonate with every woman, because, as will be discussed in chapter two, all women are made for spiritual motherhood, whether they are biological mothers or not.

The chapters are intentionally kept short so that they won't take too long to get through—roughly the length of a long article you might read online. Few mothers have a lot of time to wade through a big book. Think of them as espresso shots for the soul. (What mom doesn't need coffee?)

Christ has promised not to remove our burdens, but to make them light (see Matthew 11:28-30). Each soul is given the very circumstances that will help her get to heaven. We can't strive to become holy while also rejecting the necessary occasions that will lead us to that goal. Given our broken humanity, we much prefer an easier course: to run downhill with the wind at our backs or to just have someone else do it for us. "Isn't there a pill for that?" Ultimately, however, this passivity leads to deep boredom, depression, and listlessness.

The end of each chapter has a few reflection questions for integrating some of the ideas of this book into your own life. These can be done in a group setting or through private journaling, or you may simply consider them when doing the dishes or some other mundane activity. God has gifted us all with a unique vocation, and the more we understand ourselves, the easier it is to hear that call.

Anything worth doing *is* going to be difficult—learning a language, growing a garden, furthering our careers—but the difficulty is usually accompanied by rewarding moments or beautiful vistas, and the preciousness of our children makes the arduous transformation of ourselves worth every ounce of blood, sweat, and tears. Motherhood is not merely a quick phase to endure until we can "have our life back," but a much deeper gift.

It is a divine makeover, forming us for eternity.

ONE

Asking the Ultimate Questions

*The most beautiful women I've ever known have deep
lines on their faces, a crown of gray on their heads, and
eyes that reflect the wisdom of a noble and loving soul.*

—Denise C. McAllister[6]

Many of us live our lives one step at a time, just trying to get
through the day, without giving much thought to the big picture. Sure, we think about our careers, our families, and what
sorts of things we want to have, but when it comes to thinking
about the type of women we want to become, not so much.

Thinking about the end of our lives and what we would
like to look back upon has a way of crystallizing the most important values of our lives. Few people nearing the end of
their lives regret that they didn't work more, exercise more,
or spend more time shopping. Instead, the regrets of the past
center largely upon relationships—relationships that should
be stronger or even those that never were. Barbara Walters,
who broke through the glass ceiling of broadcast journal-
ism, recently confessed that her greatest regret in life, despite
countless awards and accolades, was that she didn't have more
children. Thinking about death, and what we want to remember when we reach our seventies and eighties and beyond, can

have a clarifying effect on what we do now. We have to ask ourselves the ultimate question: What kind of woman do I want to become?

A Good Woman Is Hard to Find

Many years ago, I met an enchanting woman. Mary, a widow most lovingly called Mamoo, was in her eighties, with white hair, a face full of wrinkles, and a figure that could envelop several small grandchildren at once. Her expansive home with a beautiful chapel on Chesapeake Bay was a haven for her sprawling family, people on retreat, and various hangers-on (like me) who just couldn't get enough of Mamoo. Her laugh was infectious and despite her advanced age, she was child-like and fun. While she had shed what had been her physical charms, she had an effervescent beauty that all who knew her wanted to be around and soak up. Mamoo's wisdom, it was clear from her life well lived, had not come from agonizing over whether she "had it all."

It is difficult to find wise women like Mamoo anymore—women who can draw the best out of anyone; who anticipate the needs of others; who are gracious and warm and funny and fun without the slightest bit of self-absorption; women who live in deep gratitude for their many blessings.

Recently I've been looking for Mamoo's deep character in women of a similar age. It is hard to find. Among the many women I've met who have reached that age, few have come close. One woman at Mass voiced concern that there weren't enough female Eucharistic servers on the altar. Another was fixated on her figure and Botoxing away her wrinkles. A third bemoaned the sad state of the world today, blaming it on interracial marriage. After picking my jaw up off the ground in response to the third, I found myself saddened that clearly despite their age, these women did not possess wisdom, but had latched on to some sort of -*ism*: feminism, ageism, and the adulation of youth, racism, whatever. It also made me sad for my children, that they will not grow up knowing that they can readily find women of a certain age to be a source of guidance, insight, and deep character—true examples to emulate. But what has happened to women like Mamoo? Why are they hard to find? Because too many women today, for one reason or another, have been convinced to place personal comfort and ambition above love, above the transformative power of having children and raising them to be happy, healthy, and holy adults. Our culture is pro-lifestyle, not pro-life.

Scripture makes it clear how important motherhood is for the soul of a woman. "Yet she shall be saved through childbearing; if she continues in faith, and love, and sanctification, with sobriety" (1 Timothy 2:9–15). One Scripture scholar points out that the Greek word for childbearing used in the original—*teknogia*—doesn't just refer to becoming pregnant or giving birth, but goes much further: it means the active and concrete reality of a woman in the home raising her children.[7] Wisdom and grace don't happen overnight, but unfold naturally as a woman experiences the many seasons of her life.

Centuries from now, historians will look back and see the twentieth century as the age when women forgot what it means to be a woman. In our drive to be "free" rather than get to the core of femininity, women have simply adopted the male vocation; it is reflected in our education, wardrobe, comportment, language, and many fashions of the day (and if it isn't masculine, the trends run toward the hyper-sexualized version of womanhood, with very little in between). It is considered well beyond the boundaries of decorum bordering on insulting to suggest that women should be anything other than outspoken, ambitious, and independent. Every occupation that was exclusive to men has been opened to women, even in the military and firefighting, though fitness tests have been shaved down to make it possible for women to pass. Most Christian denominations have changed their centuries-old rules to accommodate women who feel called to the priesthood and to serve as bishops. Now that we have made it clear that we can do almost anything men can, there are few voices asking, "What really is the heart of a woman and what is our own vocation? Is it simply to try to be like men?"

Women benefit greatly from strong role models. Given our ability to focus on small details and our propensity to constantly compare ourselves with other women, finding other women to emulate is important. It has been pointed out recently that women benefit significantly when the Church emphasizes the life of the Virgin Mary as the *ideal woman* because she provides a clear image of holiness for us to follow. Catherine Tkacz, a theology professor at the Ukrainian

Catholic University, has explained that not only is much lost theologically when we give up our devotion to Our Lady, but it leads to the dramatic confusion we see now about the role of women and even what it means to be a woman.[8]

Finding It All

Of late, there has been unending infighting among women about having it all. The largely missed question is "What kind of woman do I want to become?" or "What can I do to develop my character and become a woman of stunning beauty that radiates from my interior life even after eighty?" The debate is so fixated on the material and immediate aspects of life that the question of long-term character doesn't make it to the table. (Evidence that this debate is ill-founded is that the nuns have yet to chime in. Imagine: "You think you have it bad—we can't even leave our cloister! We can't have kids! And have you seen our outfits? Same thing. Every day.")

Despite all this, there is something unique to the woman who embraces her motherhood and the demands of raising children and serving her family joyfully that cannot be acquired through any job outside the home (even if she does also work outside the home). Every few years, a new movie comes out about a self-absorbed woman who, given some odd twist of fate, finds herself the guardian of a child, as in *Raising Helen* and *No Reservations*. The plot of these films follows the same path: Through the demands of caring for a child, the self-centered woman is transformed into someone she never dreamed she could be. This story is nothing new; in fact, it is played out every day, but not usually in the "instant" version portrayed by Hollywood. It is the life of every mother. The transformation for most of us, however, happens much more slowly and is hard to capture in a ninety-minute film. It involves countless little changes to the habits that made life work before children. Little by little, a woman is drawn out of herself and drawn into the world of caring for others.

When he was still a bishop, Pope St. John Paul II included this key phrase in one of the Vatican II documents: "Man, who is the only creature on earth that God willed for its own sake, cannot fully find himself except through a sincere gift of self."[9] That one sentence is perhaps the most profound sentence ever written. But what does that mean? The secret to life is not to spend so much time focused on ourselves. If we look there, like a dog chasing his tail, we will never find our happiness, and ironically we will never find ourselves.

Most women understand this to a certain degree, but they only want to apply it so far. Most of us could do without being woken up many times a night, confounded by disobedient children, flummoxed by teenagers, or overwhelmed by the endless slog of laundry and cleaning. And yet, it is through all of these things that we find ourselves, when we humbly accept them for the good of our children and our family and when that humble spirit of service is allowed to grow and spread internally. This is the secret Mamoo knew, and every other woman before her and since who is graced with wisdom, charity, love, and hope. Motherhood puts a woman in the perfect place to grow in holiness, whether she knows it or not, through the growth of the virtues.

The Transforming Power of Love

Women will go a long way and make a lot of sacrifices for those things they want badly enough—think of the amount of pain or sacrifice we are willing to endure to lose weight, tone the abs, have a dream house, or conceive and give birth to a child. But it is difficult to see how spiritual pain and struggle can have real value and transforming power. Sadly, there are plenty of examples of vicious mothers. True transformation requires a conscious effort on the part of the mother to grow beyond the woman she was before she got the name Mom.

Mamoo's secret and that of every beautiful woman who came before her is to recognize that "there is no real charity without detachment and self-renunciation. As love deepens through trial, so its capacity for sacrifice grows stronger."[10] This is the power of love. This power, however, isn't just about giving of oneself; it has a hidden reward. Yes, women have a unique capacity to endure difficult situations, but they are able to simultaneously experience great joy. In the face of suffering, a mother can live in both joy and peace in her steady spirit and not be overcome with agitation or restlessness.

The old rite of Christian marriage used for weddings before the Second Vatican Council has a very helpful line: "Sacrifice is usually difficult and irksome. Only love can make it easy, and perfect love can make it a joy. We are willing to give in proportion as we love. And when love is perfect, the sacrifice is complete."[11] Herein lies the secret of motherhood: Joy, pain, sacrifice, and love all grow together. The deeper the sacrifices, the greater the love, the stronger the joy.

In his insightful book *Man Enough*, Dr. Frank Pittman remarks: "These guys who fear becoming a father don't understand that fathering is not something perfect men do, but something that perfects the man. The end product of child-raising is not the child but the parent."[12] And truly, the same could be said for every woman. Parenthood offers us the opportunity to grow in perfect love, sacrifice, and joy—all wrapped up in the same package.

Questions for Reflection

1. What would you like to see when you look back on your life at age eighty?

2. Think of the women in your life whom you admire. What are some of the qualities that make them good women?

3. What do you find is the biggest impediment to living out these qualities in your own life?

TWO

The Feminine Vocation Part I: What Is Unique to Women

Women don't need to imitate men,
but simply to be themselves.

—André Feuillet[13]

My young daughter recently asked, "What can I do as a girl that is better than boys?" I confess, I struggled with how to respond. After I gave her a very poor answer, the question stayed with me. *There seems to be so much, but why can't I give her a good answer?* I thought to myself. Well, because we don't focus much on what women are uniquely gifted to do.

We have all heard the story of the wedding feast at Cana, in which Mary noticed that the wine had run out at the wedding reception and enlisted the help of Christ to fix the problem. But perhaps we have never heard it as an icon of the feminine genius:

Mary at the wedding of Cana in her quiet, observing look surveys everything and discovers what is lacking. Before anything is noticed, even before embarrassment sets in, she has procured already the remedy. She finds ways and means, she gives necessary directives, doing all quietly. She draws no attention to herself.[14]

It is hard to know what the feminine genius is or what is even unique about the female soul. So much time has been spent in the past century clearing the way for women to do whatever they wish, come what may, that any deep discussion of femininity is dismissed as passé. While not to denigrate these advances, it seems important to give women some understanding of what it means to be female beyond our lady parts.

For more than five thousand years, there have been numerous lists and explanations of the virtues, such as pride, humility, patience, prudence, etc. These lists, however important and useful, all seem to have one small problem: They were written with men in mind and not specifically tailored to the virtues of women. This lapse makes it difficult to really get to the heart of a woman—her strengths and her weaknesses. However, a great service has been done for Christian women from an unlikely source: a Jewish philosopher. Edith Stein (1891–1942) has been called the most influential German woman of the twentieth century. She was a philosopher at a time when there were few females in the field and wrote extensively about what it means to be a woman. She later converted to Catholicism and became a Carmelite nun, St. Teresa Benedicta of the Cross. Her life and genius came to a premature end when she was martyred at Auschwitz during the Second World War.

Stein made it clear that women have both a different type of body and a different kind of soul than men by citing the basic principle of St. Thomas Aquinas: *anima forma corporis*, meaning the soul is in the form of the body. To follow five thousand years of thought on the topic of gender, whatever the current trends may say, there has never been a spectrum of gender, but simply two: male and female. Contemporary culture has mistaken brokenness for identity, and sadly many who suffer from gender confusion will remain mired in their unhappy circumstances for decades to come because of our willful blindness to their wounds. It is no coincidence that we are witnessing a crisis of gender when women have made every effort to be like men and forgotten their own unique and critical calling (and while men are sliding in the opposite direction toward us).

Stein explains further that while women and men share a fundamental human nature, because women's bodies, abilities, and interests are different from men's, "a differing type of soul must exist as well."[15] Women have a uniquely feminine soul to match their uniquely feminine body. Hips, thighs, breasts—everything in our body is directed at motherhood, right down to our elbows, which are bent differently than men's to perfectly cradle a baby. (To see, hold your arms out straight, with palms up. They are angled slightly, while men's are straight.) Why should we believe that our souls are not similarly formed?

While it is the case that not every woman becomes a natural mother, every woman is called to spiritual motherhood. Stein made it clear that motherhood, at its core, meets the greatest yearning of every woman's heart: to use her gifts to bring goodness and life to others. Every woman wants to see the wholeness of her mind, body, and soul, while also contributing to the wholeness of those around her. This maternal instinct can be smudged and damaged because of sin or abuse, but is alive and well in a woman with a healthy soul. A woman's "body and soul are fashioned less to fight and to conquer than to cherish, guard and preserve."[16] Women have a natural inclination, Stein explains, to "embrace that which is living, personal, and whole. To cherish, guard, protect, nourish and advance growth is her natural, maternal yearning."[17]

And because she wants to see every being around her develop fully, she concerns herself with "the creation of an ambiance, of order and beauty conducive to their development."[18] Beauty and order are essential for a woman because they provide the right environment for other souls to grow properly.

To put Stein's idea in more concrete terms: Have you ever hosted or attended a home product party? Whoever came up with this was a genius. Perhaps Mary Kay? It takes the best of women and uses it to sell a product. What woman hosting the party doesn't want to support her friend's business and pass along to her other friends the excitement she has about a new product? Here the feminine genius is on display—women helping those they love through the powerful resource of goodwill and hospitality. (This same model does not, however, generally work for men.) While adding the feminine touch to a business is a recent innovation, this is what women have been doing for centuries.

Montessori schools offer another witness of the feminine genius at work. Maria Montessori, a forerunner in education, discovered the language of a child by listening carefully. Starting with impoverished children thought too stupid to learn, Maria found a way to teach them well beyond the experts' expectations. Part of the teaching key she discovered was to provide beautiful materials for the children to soak up and learn to respect, thereby discovering their own abilities.

There is no love without self-sacrifice, and women have a great ability to love through sacrifice. Christ highlighted this in his parable of the widow's mite, in which the impoverished widow gave from her want and not her surplus (Luke 21:1–4). Women are able to live out the example of Mary and Jesus in offering their lives for others, an agape love, in every small way throughout the day. Fr. Feuillet, a French priest who lived in the twentieth century, explained that women, at heart, "fulfill themselves by giving something of their own life so that others may live."[19]

This combination of being open to others, having an intuitive understanding of them, and the ability to sacrifice self prepares women in a unique way for spiritual and biological mothering. "When dealing with the poor and with those deprived of livelihood, their compassion is ordinarily far more inventive and efficacious than that of the masculine world," Fr. Feuillet observed.[20] Women, armed with empathy, notice the very small things that can make a big difference when others are suffering: a warm smile, a listening ear, a hot meal. While these may not solve the bigger problem, they edify and support those in the midst of struggle.

A woman's mind and intellectual life also have a different cast. While women are generally capable of mastering any skill set, their thoughts in doing so are generally directed at the whole. A woman's mind is "not so much conceptual and analytical as it is directed intuitively and emotionally to the concrete."[21] Stein argues that even if a woman finds herself in a position as a philosopher, an engineer, or a rocket scientist, her focus will likely include the big picture in a way it does not for men in the field. She will generally be motivated by how these fields can improve the lives of real people or real communities instead of simply by the science or concepts behind them.

Several years ago, I witnessed a debate at a philosophy conference between five men and a religious sister that left a deep impression. Although I have no recollection of the topic, what is etched in my memory is the jousting going on among the men as they tried to score intellectual points through their carefully worded rebuttals, while the sister was focused on trying to get a clear picture of the issue, diagnose it, then treat it. She wanted to see the whole picture. Meanwhile the men were trying to argue through it, solving the problem by coming up with the best rebuttal to their critics. While it was clear to me that each approach has its merits, it was fascinating to see men and women coming at one problem from such distinctively different angles.

Mary, Not Martha

Perhaps the most interesting piece of women's nature is the importance of interiority. Fr. Feuillet says, "The mystery of woman is above all an interior one; it shares in the interiority of the mystery of the divine Spirit."[22] No amount of busy-ness can replace the vital depths needed to find the "living water" available to a woman with an interior life. Martha learned this well when Jesus pointed out to her that Mary had chosen the better portion by resting in his presence.

There is an odd passage in Scripture about women that is hard to understand: "[F]or this reason a woman should have a sign of authority on her head, because of the angels" (1 Corinthians 11:10). Most translators suggest that head covering was merely a trend of the time, and that we need not pay attention to it anymore. Others recommend that women's heads be covered to show our submission to our husbands. One author offers an entirely different and more compelling argument, particularly if one looks at the original translations (which we are not going to do): The woman is veiled because of the intrinsic, God-given ability women have to be close to God, to hear his voice, and to pass along his words to others (no one can doubt our ability to spread the word). The veil is a sign of her relationship to God, which, as part of the feminine nature, is meant to be hidden, quiet, intimate, and open to hearing the wisdom of the Lord. A woman's spiritual function, "like that of the Virgin, is sublime, but it is hidden, just as the formation of a child in the mother's womb is hidden."[23]

Women have a strong sense of interiority because it is there that God speaks most directly to them. A woman, Stein explains, is able to "collect her forces in silence."[24] Her strength comes from her deep connection to the living water from God. Like Mary Magdalene's, our fallen feminine nature can be restored to its purity with a complete surrender to God. "When we entrust all the troubles of our earthly existence confidently to the divine heart, we are relieved of them. Then our soul is free to participate in the divine life."[25] Like he promised the woman at the well, Christ comes to us in a unique way in living water that feeds our soul.

Meanwhile, however, secular feminists entreat women to act like busy Marthas, berating those of us who dare to consider the virtues of Mary. And yet, how many of us thirst to hear God's voice? To know his will for our lives? To get hints and glimmers that not only is the Creator of the universe speaking to *me*, but he has an actual plan and mission for my life?

Women Who Work Outside the Home

Stein, in her work on women, spoke extensively about working women. At the time, her own country of post–World War I Germany was facing severe economic conditions and many women had to work simply for survival. She makes it clear that women are certainly capable of most any profession, but given the feminine cast of mind and heart there may be professions to which women are better suited. Regardless, because of their feminine nature, women will generally bring different skills and perspectives to work than men do. Stein, in fact, was a promoter of what she called solid, objective work, whether it be a profession or even waitressing tables. She saw that hard work was a "natural remedy against all typical feminine defects."[26] Work requires women to move beyond their own self-absorption and superficial interests, while it also provides an education in obedience "because it requires submission to objective laws."[27]

Stein does acknowledge the difficulty of juggling family and full-time work. "Therein arises the difficult problem of the double vocation: there is danger that her work outside the home will so take over that finally it can make it impossible for her to be the heart of the family and the soul of the home, which must always remain her essential duty."[28] This can be a very difficult balance in our own culture, where much of our identity is based on what we do, instead of who we are and the person God created us to be.

Regardless of our circumstances, the Holy Spirit is infinitely creative and new: He works with various personalities for the good of a family, which might include non-traditional situations such as single motherhood following the death of a husband or the decision to have a father stay home with the children when a woman's career is more lucrative. There are countless examples of saints who lived unusual lives steeped in great holiness. Sociologist W. Bradford Wilcox, in his research on contemporary women, has found that those who report being the happiest are stay-at-home mothers who also have some kind of part-time work beyond the home.[29] It is an interesting mix of the old and the new, but a surprising one if you consider the strong feminist voices decrying the "wasted" time of staying home with your children.

Stein makes it clear that authentic feminine happiness, regardless of the contemporary trends, hinges upon our union with God. "Whether she is a mother in the home, or occupies a place in the limelight of public life, or lives behind quiet cloister walls, she must be a handmaid of the Lord everywhere."[30] Being his handmaid, simply stated, involves seeking out his will for our lives in all things while growing in love and sacrifice for others through our own talents.

Questions for Reflection

1. How would you describe the feminine vocation?

2. What examples can you think of in your own life, community, and experience that embody the feminine vocation?

3. What aspects of the feminine vocation are most attractive to you?

THREE

The Feminine Vocation Part II: Bridging Heaven and Earth

An ounce of mother is worth a pound of priests.

—Spanish Proverb

When I was a graduate student, a male friend of mine did me the greatest favor, although at the time it didn't feel like it. He actively pointed out to me when I was acting in a way that was crazy making to men. After spending years learning to compete with men in any arena, it never occurred to me that there could be a feminine way to act. While I bristled at first from his insights, they began to sink in.

Several years later I discovered a book called *Fascinating Womanhood*.[31] I had never seen anything like it—it said the *exact opposite* of everything I had ever been taught as a female. This little book written in the 1960s, which has sold more than two million copies, laid out the very basic claims that 1) women need to respect their husbands and their authority as the head of the household, and 2) men need the admiration of their wives for their own sense of self-worth. When this order is upset, men, feeling as though the wind has been taken from their sails, disengage from their marriage in one way or another. My intrigue with the book only deepened after I witnessed a marriage saved when the wife applied its advice. And while this sounds like perhaps a bridge too far in our own day and age, bear with me.

The Bridge

One name for the pope is "pontiff," which is a derivation of the word *pontifex*, or "bridge builder"—the pope is the link, or bridge, between God and the Church. Similarly, mothers are called to be bridges linking their families to God. Mary, in her yes to God to bear Jesus, is the female bridge through which man has been linked back to God. What Eve demolished, Mary restored. The Old Testament is riddled with stories of heroic women, such as Esther and Ruth, but with Mary's yes (her *fiat*), women took on a more specific role. The significant events related to Christ were first made known to women; for example, Elizabeth announced the Incarnation of God through the leap of John in her womb, while Mary Magdalene was the first to encounter Christ after his Resurrection. These women were given great insights that they carried in their hearts, while waiting for the good news to be heralded by others.

Throughout the centuries, this pattern of a holy woman having an insight and then patiently waiting for men to act has repeated itself again and again: when St. Catherine of Siena convinced Pope Gregory XI to leave Avignon, France, and return to Italy; when St. Bernadette told her bishop that the lady at the spring was the Immaculate Conception; and when St. Thérèse confidently asked her bishop to allow her to enter Carmel before she had reached the required age. This is not to say that the insights of the faith always come through women; it's just to emphasize a familiar route through which God frequently works.

These roles of men and women, in which a woman receives the message and then the man acts, are illustrated with Adam and Eve, but with a dark twist. Satan, who ever distorts the order God set up, first approaches Eve and convinces her to eat the forbidden fruit, and then Adam passively goes along with her suggestion. This sad abandonment of masculine authority first witnessed with Adam and Eve is also evidenced in the New Testament. Herodias, the wife of Herod, who asks for St. John the Baptist's head on a platter, embodies an Eve character. Through manipulation, she demands something from her husband, and he finds himself in a bind, obligated to serve up St. John's head because of his own cowardice. Rather than embodying the voice of Mary, who said at the wedding feast at Cana, "Do whatever he tells you," Herodias is an anti-Mary: "Do what whatever *I* tell you" (although she doesn't say it literally).

In our own culture, Eve's fingerprints are everywhere. Over and over again in our families, women usurp the active role of men, making authoritative decisions without them or overruling them, while the men passively resign, unwilling to engage in another battle of wills. Rather than being the bridge between heaven and earth, the wife in this case, like Eve, is the bridge between earth and hell.

In Ephesians 5, a path for a family to pursue the bridge from earth to heaven is laid out very clearly. It is no surprise that this passage has become so controversial that parishes are provided an alternative so they don't have to read the contentious bits.

> Wives should be subordinate to their husbands as to the Lord. For the husband is head of his wife just as Christ is head of the church, he himself the savior of the body. As the church is subordinate to Christ, so wives should be subordinate to their husbands in everything. (Ephesians 5:22–24)

Hard stuff for modern ears, but it lines up perfectly with the example of Mary and every holy woman before and after who knows the hidden door to getting her family to heaven.

What is usually overlooked, however, is the part just before this that says, "Be subordinate to one another out of reverence for Christ" (Ephesians 5:21), and then "Husbands, love your wives, even as Christ loved the church and handed himself over for her to sanctify her" (Ephesians 5:25). We all know how Christ loved the Church—by offering his life on the cross. Husbands, in fact, have the much harder task, once you consider what the passage actually says. It continues:

> So also husbands should love their wives as their own bodies. He who loves his wife loves himself. For no one hates his own flesh but rather nourishes and cherishes it,

even as Christ does the church, because we are members of his body. (Ephesians 5:28–30)

It is the *mutual* subordination that creates harmony, holiness, and fruitfulness in a couple's relationship and creates the icon—a true image—of the Trinity: the Father, the Son, and the Holy Spirit, a third person created by the mutual love between the Father and the Son. Or the husband, the wife, and the third person created by their mutual love: the child.

Got Your Back

We have all heard the out-of-fashion line "Behind every great man, there has to be a great woman." But I think the opposite is also true. Women need the support of men just as much as men need women, despite what secular feminists may tell us. While there are overwhelming examples of women who have made do without men, until recently, it was generally not a chosen path, but the result of some kind of misfortune. Our wealth has given us the impression that it can be done easily, but even this is a historical anomaly.

While many people view it as terribly old-fashioned to have a father walk his daughter down the aisle to be handed off to her husband, this act underlines something important about the feminine heart: The soul of a woman matures and is able to take flight, or truly love others in her own unique way, when she has the keen awareness that she is loved, first by her father and then by her husband. The loving union she has with these men, one often a precursor to the next (for better or worse), is very important when it comes to her own ability to love. In her book *Strong Fathers, Strong Daughters*,[32] pediatrician Meg Meeker makes it absolutely clear the influence a father will have on a daughter's life, for good or for ill. For this reason, many women struggle with a "father wound," remaining unsure of themselves in tangible ways and choosing husbands who reflect it.

This idea of being able to surrender oneself to the support of a loving father is also evident in spiritual motherhood. Those women who vow to give their lives as the bride of Christ as a religious sister, cloistered nun, or consecrated virgin make a total self-surrender to God. This is not to say that a married woman doesn't surrender to God—certainly she must—but her union with her husband is the avenue through which God shows his love for her, while providing a platform for her to give her love and care to those around her. Women need to know that a man has her back, whether a father, a husband, or in the case of religious, through the members of the Trinity.

We see this model in the relationship between the Church and its hierarchy—the pope, bishops, and priests. The Church is represented as a woman—a mother—while the men have a paternal role, acting in the place of Christ. Together, like the married couple, the two draw a beautiful icon of God.

Within this relationship to a man, a woman's body and soul take on similar tasks. Physically, she becomes pregnant and a child is hidden until birth. The same is true of a woman's soul. God plants treasures in her heart, allowing them to grow and become stronger, and then finally, when it is time for them to bear fruit, they do. You hear women who have started important and life-giving initiatives talk this way over and over again. Joanna Gaines, a mother of four and interior designer on HGTV's *Fixer Upper*, explained how she had to give up on one project but that God told her in prayer he would give her a bigger platform. Admitting that she scarcely knew what this meant, she just trusted and years later she now has one of the most popular home shows on TV. First the idea is planted and later the reality is born. Meanwhile she is supported by Chip, her husband, who doesn't have the same insights, but who helps to execute her vision once she makes clear to him what it is. Throughout the process Joanna makes it clear that she adores and respects her husband.

Simply put, spiritually through prayer, God plants treasures in our souls. Women are then responsible for nourishing, feeding, and taking care of them, even when they are still very hidden, and then finally acting on them when the time is right. For decades Mother Teresa nourished her vocation that would later unfold as the global order of the Missionaries of Charity.

Pointing Out the Path to Heaven

For several years after I was married, it bothered me that I was usually the one to suggest praying a Rosary or going to daily Mass, not my husband. It finally occurred to me that this, too, is part of a woman's calling. She is the transmitter of the faith.

While the husband plays a different role, she is the one to plant those first seeds. In the same way she is receptive to the grace of God in the seeds he plants in her soul, she is then able to spread these seeds to others. Here again, we see the core of the feminine genius: She opens herself to God's grace and then is able to pass it on to others.

Pope Francis has made this unique role of women a recurrent theme in his homilies and audiences, reminding us of women's fundamental duty to assist their children to become saints. It is women who first impart divine love to the souls of their children: "It is the path chosen by Jesus. He wanted to have a mother: the gift of faith comes to us through women, as Jesus came to us through Mary."[33] The pope further explains:

> Mothers also often transmit the profoundest meaning of religious practice. The value of the faith is inscribed in the life of a human being in the first prayers, in the first gestures of devotion that a child learns. It is a message that believing mothers are able to transmit without explanations: these will come later, but the seed of the faith is in those first, most precious moments.[34]

I know a man from Ukraine who grew up under the rigid and brutal Communist regime. His grandmother baptized him in secret when he was still just a boy and quietly taught him the faith, unbeknownst even to his parents. Today, he is a priest. Without this quiet and courageous gift from his grandmother, his faith may never have blossomed. She risked her life to pass her faith on to him.

But faith can't be handed on if you don't have it. We cannot give what we don't have. Like the wise virgins from the parable of the ten virgins waiting for the bridegroom to arrive (Matthew 25:1–13), we must fill our lamps with oil; that is, we must be open to the grace God and Our Lady wish to pour into our souls—and then share it with others. Without our receptivity to God's grace, we will bear no fruit.

The Mystery of Women

There is something mysterious about women; it has been a topic of fascination from time immemorial. The countless portraits of beautiful women over the centuries capture something contemplative in the feminine soul, even in the smile of the *Mona Lisa*. Few men in their odes of love have ever written, "I love her for the way she nags me! Oh, the pantsuits! And the salary she brings in from making such important decisions in the boardroom." Rather, they grapple with language to pinpoint the elusive essence of the fairer sex. In reality, it is her goodness, her ability to give herself freely to others, her smile and gentleness—the emanations from her very soul—that are the allure.

A look at poetry and music reveals the deep esteem men have for women, but as the verses and lyrics make clear, women have an enigmatic tenderness and depth of soul that moves their hearts. Even the music of 1970s folk guru James

Taylor captures the difficulty men have in pinpointing exactly what it is about the woman they love that moves them so deeply. And although James Taylor would likely consider himself to a promoter of the modern woman, he and every other poet and songsmith before him have certainly described a woman in terms much deeper, more beautiful, and more compelling than the picture given of most women today about the power and beauty of their souls.

Women were made to be enchanting—to help the world to understand that their beauty and the wonder it elicits point to something beyond themselves. It is not meant simply for the viewing pleasure of men, but as the bridge that they willingly fly over to be united to both the beautiful and the artist behind it—the Divine Artist. Secular culture has reduced the allure of women solely to their sexuality, and yet, the true enigma of a woman is in the power of her *soul*: her intuition, her gentle care for others, even the logic that sometimes only her heart understands.

Often, it can be difficult for us as women to understand why God made us the way he did, or what is so distorted with our current understanding of what it means to be female. Scripture scholar Fr. Feuillet explains:

> If Adam, coming forth from the hands of the Creator, is instinctively attached to Eve, it is because he discovers in her the completion of that image of God which is himself—she is, in a word, a manifestation of the love that Creator had for him. In mirroring to Adam his

own image, which is an image of God, Eve turns Adam toward God; her role is to turn Adam not only toward herself, but also toward God.[35]

When women are allowed to be women, and men can be men, and both sexes understand their mutual submission to Christ and each other, women are freest, happiest, and most fulfilled. This is because when man and woman renounce themselves and turn toward God, they become more of what they already are—the image of God.[36]

Questions for Reflection

1. In what ways do you bridge heaven and earth for your family?

2. Are there other areas of your relationships that you can improve upon to help others to know God?

3. Can you think of other examples from history, literature, or your own experience that reveal the bridge-building capacity of women?

FOUR

Virtues 101:
The Source of Happiness

Everything in this world is precarious. Health,
riches, power and talents are all uncertain.
Virtue alone is subject to no vicissitudes.

—Charles Carroll of Carrollton, signer of the
Declaration of Independence, after the death of his son[37]

I've always loved archeology, or at least the idea of it. The thought of finding some hidden treasure from the past, dusting it off, and cleaning it up for the rest of the world to learn about has fascinated me since childhood. I never dreamed, however, that this love would find a place in my life as a philosopher. It took me fifteen years to get my doctorate in philosophy—plenty of time to wade through dense and tedious texts, but among the pages and pages, I unearthed an old treasure of great worth. I have discovered the well-kept secret of the ancient Greeks and medieval philosophers: the virtues. Far from being bland and prudish throwbacks to the Victorian era, virtues are a key to happiness. Let me dust them off a bit and show you what I mean.

The study of virtues has a long and brilliant history. Dating back to ancient Greece, virtues were considered by philosophers of the day to be vital to happiness. Christian philosophers took these important tools and baptized them, so to speak, by organizing them in light of Christ's teachings. For fifteen hundred years the virtues were touted by the Church as the fundamental avenue to happiness and holiness. Even to this day, the Catholic Church still uses them as the standard for determining if a person's life was worthy of canonization, giving them the title of saint. Unfortunately, however, because of major shifts in philosophy, theology, and culture, the virtues were largely tossed aside as unimportant. The new standard moral codes became variations of doing one's duty in the eighteenth and nineteenth centuries and were then followed by the trendy notion of rights in the twentieth century. While among academics the virtues have been experiencing something of a renaissance, their usefulness and potential have yet to trickle back down to the average Catholic in the pew.[38]

What Are the Virtues?

A quick look at a list of virtues holds little appeal: meekness, prudence, frugality. The list sounds more like a Jane Austen novel than a recipe for happiness. Put aside any preconceived ideas you have about these terms that bring up notions of wallflowers and milquetoasts. These mistaken stereotypes have precious little to do with the reality of virtues lived out in daily life.

The virtues, in essence, are tools we have been given by God to help us find happiness. Not happiness defined simply as having pleasant experiences or the absence of suffering. That is hedonism. But a kind of happiness that stamps our lives with two unmistakable hallmarks, even in the face of suffering: peace and joy.

In short, the definition of a virtue is: an innate potential in a person that through repeated use becomes a habit, freeing her to do what she knows is good, true and beautiful while bringing out the best of her character. Let me break it down for you.

First, a virtue is *an innate potential within a person.* When lifting weights, a woman at the gym does not think, "I sure hope I have biceps." If her body is not damaged, then of course she knows she has biceps. They may be small, and they may hurt a lot after doing too many curls, but that only confirms that she has biceps, however weak. Virtues are the muscles of our character. We know we have patience. We may have very little of it, and it may sting when we're forced to use it, but we can be assured it is there, ready to be used when necessary. All the virtues are like the muscles. When not used, they are weak, but when tapped, after the initial pain they become strong and nimble.

As with improving the health of your body through exercise, the health of the soul can't be improved passively. No one gets fit by being a couch potato. So, too, no one gets to be virtuous without making the effort to do so. Imagine the athlete who says, "I really want to go to the Olympics next year, but I have to find a way to do it without training." We would know immediately that this person is not going to be up on the podium receiving a medal. It simply cannot happen. So, too, with the saint. "I want to go to heaven but not work at it" is just as nonsensical as our lazy Olympian's statement.

If we were perfectly virtuous, motherhood would be a snap. When we are struggling, the pain points to our weakness, showing us what virtues we need to work on. This is a whole new way of looking at the pain. Instead of just seeing laughter or chocolate as our only escape from our frustrations and difficulties (and don't get me wrong—I like both options), we find that something deeper is at work. The Marines have a saying: "Pain is weakness leaving the body." The pain we experience when straining for virtue is from the vice leaving our character.

Often, people will say they just don't have the patience for more children. Actually, like biceps, the patience is there unless it's somehow damaged—it just needs strengthening. This is why, for most of us, motherhood is so difficult—simply because it flexes muscles we aren't accustomed to flexing. How many of us grew up with young siblings or small children we had to look after? Even babysitting jobs we may have had usually didn't entail long hours with small children. Instead, most of us were raised in homes with one or two children, and then in our educational and professional lives, few social demands were placed upon us to be attentive to the needs of others, much less little others. Yes, there are certainly some women who temperamentally are better suited to being mothers, but that doesn't mean that being a good mother can't be learned and the skills acquired.

Many people believe they have a fixed character that can't be changed. "This is just the way I am." While clearly there are personality distinctions discernible from birth, there is little reason to believe that our moral character is fixed. It can just feel that way because of the weakness of our virtues or the comfort of our vices.[39]

Second, a virtue *through repeated use becomes a habit.* Again, like the muscles of the body, when used the same way over and over again, the muscles of our character acquire muscle memory—like the reflexes of a tennis player at the net who doesn't even have to think as she returns a quick volley. A virtue is a reaction born of repeated actions in the face of life's trials. It has the ability to grow or to weaken, depending on how much it is used, but only when it is used without thinking has it become a true habit of soul.

Third, a virtue is a habit that is *freeing.* No one looks at an athlete and says, "Wow, that guy can play basketball well, but I bet he gets tired of the rules of the game. Wouldn't it be better if there weren't any rules in basketball?" Would LeBron James be a better basketball player if he didn't have to follow the boundaries of the court? Would Serena Williams be a better tennis player if there were no net? Of course not—it is the rules, the structure of the game, that give the athlete the parameters within which to work.

In a similar way, God has given us the basic rules, such as the Ten Commandments and the rich teachings of the Church, to guide us to happiness, and we get to grow our habits so we can work creatively within those boundaries.

As with basketball, the skill set doesn't make sense outside the rules of the game. It is through the rules that we can actually see the skill and dexterity of a given character. The saints are those who lived heroic virtue, nimbly displaying through their lives the best way to play the game, so to speak. The saint acts in life like the musician who has mastered his instrument, who can now compose whatever he wants in new and surprising ways. Think of Bach or Mozart. Their music, to those who know them, is readily recognizable because they put their hallmark on their work. So too with the saint—many are recognizable because of their unique ways of living out their character; hence we can speak of someone with a Franciscan character, or a Dominican soul, referring to the spiritual footprints of Saints Francis and Dominic. St. Augustine said it best: "Love and do as you please." This love that mimics divine charity is a grace-filled love that leads us to act virtuously. It embodies *true* love, that of self-sacrifice and self-gift.

Fourth, virtue calls us *to do what is good, true, and beautiful.* At the heart of every soul is the desire for the good, the true, and the beautiful. Unfortunately, because we are comfortable in vice, they can often be difficult to see. We can come to love those things that are subjectively satisfying, such as pleasure, rather than truly loving those things with higher value, such as children. All vice darkens the intellect and the ability to see, know, and love God. Living with the virtues clears the clutter from our minds and opens up a world of wisdom that comes from loving the most lovable things first and leaving aside those things—pleasure, money, comfort—that are not to be pursued for their own sake.

Finally, the virtues also *bring out the best of our character.* The most vital and invigorating thing to remember about the virtues is that, far from making us just like everyone else, they make us more of who we really are, pulling out our own interior genius, revealing that unique spark that each person has. In a sense, they are the real archaeological dig—they unearth the real you. It is sin that makes us banal, boring, inhumane. We are used to seeing teenagers at the mall "expressing themselves" through piercings, smoking, dressing in dark clothes, but most of the time they look exactly like each other. Virtue is alive, creative, and unique.

The virtues, then, are the tools our souls need for happiness. They help us to draw closer to God and his will in our lives. Until we do that, our hearts will be restless and unhappy. When a person is virtuous, she is fully alive in the potential that God has given her. Think of your average day. It probably includes any number of frustrations, irritations, and struggles. For a mother, it is easy to feel like your emotions dictate how the day will go as you react to whatever comes your way through your children, over whom you don't have ultimate control, no matter what their age. The virtues are the tools that help you act and react the way that you want to instead of feeling like your life is out of your hands, out of your control. You are able to control yourself and therefore are not overcome by the winds blowing around you. The virtues are the habits of mind and soul that help you to be the best *you* in any given situation.

Pope Francis has provided a succinct and compelling description of how the virtues work:

> If we follow [the path of virtue], trials will not be so overwhelming, and the further we advance, the lighter they will appear. Indeed, as our souls grow, we become stronger and more capable of bearing everything that happens to us. Look at a beast of burden. If it is sturdy, it cheerfully carries the heavy burden that is loaded onto it; if it loses its balance it gets up straightaway and suffers no harm. If it is weak, however, any load is too much for it; and if it falls, it needs a lot of help to get back on its feet. The same is true of the soul. We are weakened every time we sin, because sin exhausts and corrupts the sinner. Anything at all is enough to overwhelm us then. But if instead we advance in virtue, what previously overcame us becomes more and more bearable. This is a great advantage to us, an abundant source of peace and progress, because it makes *us*, not other people, responsible for what happens, especially since nothing can happen to us without God's providence.[40]

And yes, while it may all sound too good to be true, being virtuous is not easy. The advantage we have as mothers is that the cost is already built into motherhood. We are already well on our way to living the virtuous life based simply upon the gift of self that we make every day to our children.

Questions for Reflection

1. In what ways has this chapter brought new light to the virtues for you?

2. How does equating the virtues with happiness change your own thoughts about what it means to be happy?

3. What virtues—perhaps that you see in others—do you admire most?

FIVE

Escaping the Crippling Habits of Vice

All of the defects in a man's nature which cause him to fail in his original vocation are rooted in a perverted relationship to God.

—Edith Stein[41]

Know thyself. These are the ancient words of Socrates that have come to us through the ages, repeated by such illustrious saints as Thomas Aquinas, Catherine of Siena, and Teresa of Ávila. There is significant spiritual value in knowing our weaknesses, or our vices. When we are unaware of our faults, we cannot correct them. And when we are unfamiliar with our gifts, we cannot use them. Self-knowledge gives us the means to change all that.

When it comes to our daily lives, we all live with original sin. There is simply no way around it. Our vices are our habitual sins, or the types of sin that come most easily to us and inhibit our relationships with others and with God, and frequently stymie our best efforts. Because they are the opposite of virtue, they limit us, deform our character, and lead to misery. Additionally, vice distorts our thinking: the more vicious we are, the more difficult it is to recognize virtue. We can also hide our vices from ourselves. Sometimes they are so habitual, we aren't even aware of them. (Although ask your spouse or perhaps a sibling about your vices. They know.)

It is possible for entire cultures to have similar virtues and vices. For example, Italy is known for the Mafia, the black market, and dishonest dealings. When I lived there, my friend's apartment came with two leases: one for the real cost and the other for the courts so the landlady could get more alimony from her ex-husband. Economic corruption is so commonplace, people think you are strange if you don't participate in it. Vice can be contagious, such that what was once repulsive becomes accepted. Flipping through the TV channels or nearly every woman's magazine will confirm this. The film and television industry crank out product after product that had they been released several decades ago the producers would have been thrown in jail. Now they are hailed as cultural icons. And because vice makes us blind to just how bad it is, we need to find other ways to free ourselves from its slavery.

One way to free ourselves from the contagion of vice is to see the virtues in those striving to live good lives. Even if there are no virtuous people around, we can still find virtue by reading literature about heroes and heroines of the past, or the lives of the saints. Books, particularly from different eras, provide a rich context and insights into characters' thoughts and motivations that are difficult to portray on a screen.

Additionally, any struggles we may have in relationships are good indicators of our vices. It is often easy to hide our faults when we're not confronted by the sandpaper of relationships or other types of adversity (changes in fortune, etc.). Often it can be difficult to imagine that there is more to us than what we have already known. Each soul has deep and familiar tracks of the same sins, the same struggles, the same wounds and frustrations, many of which we have gotten beyond and those that still prick us, sometimes unexpectedly. We frequently put limitations even on God, believing that he cannot remove our old burdens or our comfortable vices. But God, as we witness in the lives of the saints, not only helps to remove our vice; he allows our souls to be lifted out of the vicious cultures we may happen to find ourselves in, giving us a new vantage point of goodness, truth, and beauty. The saints were those who, no matter the climate around them, found higher ground. It is as if God simply extracted their spirits, pulling them out of the muck and up to that higher ground to see the world as it really is.

Harder Is Not Always Better

There have been many confusing trends in ethics over the past five hundred years. One trend that has taken root is the idea that if something is incredibly hard for us to do, then we should do it. For instance, at the beginning of Lent, we frequently give up something very difficult, such as coffee or chocolate, and then before the day is through, not only are we lamenting our sacrifice, but we have caved and are feeling defeated by not being able to give up that favorite treat (or necessity, if it's coffee). However, just because something is really hard for us to do doesn't mean that we are growing interiorly by doing it. Often we aim too high, setting ourselves up for failure, when what is really needed are almost imperceptible incremental changes.

When our virtues are growing and difficult situations arise, choosing the morally good action becomes easier, not harder. Yes, there will be times of aridity and struggle as we grow further in virtue, but generally, our growth is incremental and moving steadily forward, not a pendulum swinging from depravity to divinity. In fact, this is a characteristic of vice first outlined by Aristotle more than two millennia ago. As humans, we find it is easier for our minds to go from one extreme to the other, rather than look for what can be called the happy medium. The vices usually exist on the extremes and virtue is somewhere in the middle. The diet industry thrives because of our pendulum swings—we overeat and then try to compensate with a crash diet; meanwhile the middle way avoids both extremes.

We can see how having children helps us grow in virtue incrementally. Our children are a thing of wonder; we love them beyond belief at our first meeting. God in his mercy has given us the most gentle (and adorable) avenue to grow in virtue. Yes, we make many sacrifices for them, but with each sacrifice our love grows. While it is true that raising children is likely one of the hardest things you will ever do, there are much more difficult ways to become holy, such as martyrdom or prolonged illness. God in his mercy and love wants us to become holy, and he gives us a gentle path to get there. The sacrifice is real, but so are the joy, the peace, and the awareness that our gift is fruitful.

It is easy for us, as women, to overlook the many good things we do throughout the day, the victories already won, and focus on our weaknesses. Once you start paying attention to what the Holy Spirit is doing interiorly, old struggles will fall away and new issues will present themselves; the goalposts are moved to accommodate the new growth. The first step, however, is usually the hardest simply because you are breaking a habit—but little by little it gets easier.

In addition to being aware of our vices, there are, of course, other basic things we can do as Catholics to first repair and then grow in intimacy with God. Attending Mass, starting with every Sunday but also perhaps on weekdays, is vital. The sacraments, particularly the infinitely rich food of the Eucharist, offer us the graces to change. Mass can be challenging with children, but it can also help give them graces they need for all that life throws our way. Regular confession, a daily Rosary, and reading about the saints are also great tools. These are all good ways to help root out vice and come to know God so that we can love him. We cannot love someone we don't know, but loving someone changes everything—as every mother knows the instant she sees her child.

From Vice to Virtue

Motherhood makes it tough to hide our vices. Before having children, most women find they can mask their vices by avoiding others or situations that reveal their impatience or a short fuse. Or we deny them: "I'm just not that kind of a person." Or we reinvent them altogether: "Impatience is a virtue too!" But once you become a mother, those vices seem to be on display—at least to you: "I never knew I had so many weaknesses." And once you hit that point, God has you right where he wants you. It is much easier to reshape a woman who knows she is weak than one who is proud and unaware. God wants us to rely upon him—to give our burdens, weaknesses, and struggles back to him so he can transform them and us. Pope John XXIII used to say before going to bed at night, "Lord, it's your Church. I'm going to bed." He knew who was in charge.

Rather than discouraging us, an awareness of our vices offers important clues about what virtues we may be able to develop. For example, Judy loved to use her quick thinking to get out of anything she didn't want to do. She was a liar; she could lie about anything. She prided herself on coming up with the most outrageous lies just to see if she could get away with it. At one point in her life, a friend suggested that lying was exhausting because of the amount of memory required to recall both the truth and the lie. This made an impression on her, but not enough. Finally, Judy realized that if she wanted to get closer to God, the lies had to stop. Of course, it was hard at first, but slowly, slowly, she let go of the untruths. Meanwhile, she realized that she not only had the ability to tell the truth, but she had the courage to do it even when it was difficult. The lies were a clue to what would become one of her greatest virtues: telling the truth in love, even when it was hard. She eventually became a teacher, telling real stories to edify her students, instead of the tall tales of deception she had spun in her head.

Like Judy, we all have vices just waiting to be flipped into virtues. These terrible vices can become beautiful virtues because they are part of every woman's unique vocation—the special call that God has for each of us to do on earth. The key, of course, is to first identify these vices and then root them out and replace them with a virtue. So if you think yourself a coward, you might be, but you likely have great potential to be very courageous; if you're proud, then you can be humble; if stingy, generous; if a glutton, temperate, and so on. The difficult part is that when we are growing in virtue, the vice can still be alive and well, so our greatest virtue can also be our greatest vice—until we either struggle to gain the virtue or give in to the vice.

Moving Forward

The next four chapters focus on women's most common types of vices and their opposing virtues. This is certainly not meant to be an exhaustive list; rather, it's a general way to think about your own virtues and vices and what God might be trying to teach you.

As you read through the following lists, be mindful of your own weaknesses, as well as those you see in others. Think of women you admire in your life—what traits do you wish you had? And which ones really drive you crazy when you see them in others? Usually the vices that you find most irritating are a good indication of a vice you may have. Not always, but it is certainly worth a second and deeper look when that red flag appears.

Questions for Reflection

1. Which vices or sins come to you most easily?

2. Which vices are you most uncomfortable with when you see them in others?

3. Are these two lists similar or different? In what ways?

SIX

Pride and Perspective

*If you know these two things you will have
beatitude within your grasp. You are she
who is not, and I AM HE WHO IS.*[42]

—St. Catherine of Siena

Over the centuries, there has been much debate about the exact number of virtues and vices. As you read on, you will notice there is a lot of overlap among them that makes it difficult to put them into tidy categories. Pope Gregory the Great decided upon seven vices, what we also know today as the "seven deadly sins." One element that stands out about his list is that all of the vices revolve around the sin of pride; he doesn't even list pride as a vice because it so clearly underpins *every* vice.

Rather than consider every vice and its relationship to pride, this chapter will focus on the specific ways in which the sin of pride as a type of self-absorption manifests itself in women. Some of these vices reveal themselves in various ways for women, even to the point of appearing to be virtues—but the central problem is that they take what should naturally be an external gaze toward the needs of others and turn it on its head, making the gaze an interior one.

Vanity

We have all seen the woman who on the outside is the picture of physical perfection, but once she opens her mouth, her beauty shrinks away because of the crassness of her character. In the 1998 hit *You've Got Mail*, Tom Hanks' character, Joe Fox, is dating the quintessential successful woman, Patricia Eden—beautiful, smart, successful, ambitious. The two get stuck in an elevator where she shows her true colors, ranting and raving, and the relationship comes to an effortless end on the part of Fox. Her beauty had little depth and was simply a thin veneer to hide her vicious character.

Edith Stein keenly describes the vain woman as one who has a deep "desire for praise and recognition, and an unchecked need for communication." Her vanity doesn't settle just upon herself, but also reveals itself "in an excessive interest in others [through] curiosity, gossip, and an indiscreet need to penetrate into the intimate life of others." Stein says she "fritters away her powers" through a "superficial nibbling in all areas."[43] If this is not an apt description of our social media world, I'm not sure what is. This type of vanity is marked by an excessive busy-ness, but with very little to show for it in terms of actually producing something or forming strong bonds of deep and abiding friendship.

With motherhood, vanity is checked first and foremost by a bulging body, sagging skin, wrinkles, and stretch marks. The postpartum figure rarely returns to the prime of youth. What seemed so important—fitting into our skinny jeans—fades into the background as our energies are redirected to something far more important.

Vanity's interior gazing is the exact opposite of the gracious spirit women exude when they desire to serve others in love that comes from the virtue of humility. Having humility, derivative of the word *humus*, meaning "of the earth," or "grounded," is not simply denying one's accomplishments, but recognizing what is true about ourselves. It gives a woman the awareness of who she is, as well as what she is not. She is not the center of the world; she is made to love and serve God. These corrections to vanity, won daily in loving service to her family, come easily to moms.

Envy

Women have the ability to focus on an abundance of details. When used for the best, this data that we take in on a daily basis helps us to evaluate who needs what and how we can best use our resources. When distorted, these virtues of graciousness or empathy get turned on their head to become envy. Our culture is so saturated with envy, it almost seems natural to compare ourselves *ad nauseam* with every other woman around us. There are few things that disfigure the soul of a woman like envy and its favorite tool, gossip. Envy is that old habit that tells us we aren't enough, or that she is too much and therefore makes me look like less. Literature is full of women who have done the darkest of deeds because they wanted what someone else had, spawning all sorts of ugly scenarios of revenge, gossip, calumny, and slander.

Motherhood, on the one hand, can exacerbate envy not only because of the sacrifices involved but also because of the nagging feeling many women have that they aren't very good mothers. "Look at what she is doing. Should I be doing that?" It is easy to get carried away trying to do *everything* for our children. And yet, eventually, motherhood can bring us to that point where we say, "Enough. I simply have to do what I'm called to do, while humbly accepting that if I try to do everything, I will drive all of us crazy."

Motherhood brings a humble spirit into focus: we know that we cannot do anything without God. The challenges are just too great to leave us with the false impression that somehow we are in control of our lives. The very act of conceiving a child and the miracle of birth are reminders enough. Humility tells us that we have a mission only we can execute—and getting ensnared in spite and envy will only divert us from our real goal of becoming holy women and raising faithful children.

As for gossip, it is hard not to be pulled into its orbit. A woman can protect herself from participating in gossip by keeping her conversations candid, sincere, and truthful. It helps to also be mindful that these activities only take away our energy instead of energizing us with joy. As mothers, we have learned to adjust our attitudes to look at the needs of our children with loving concern, to let the virtue of empathy grow. It is this same shift in attitude that can transform our relationships with those beyond our homes.

The Flighty and Fickle

In season three of *Downton Abbey*, Violet Crawley, the Dowager Countess of Grantham, talks with Isobel Crawley about the demands of parenting:

> Violet: One forgets about parenthood. The on-and-on-ness of it.
> Isobel: Were you a very involved mother with Robert and Rosamund?
> Violet: Does it surprise you?
> Isobel: A bit. I'd imagined them surrounded by nannies and governesses, being starched and ironed to spend an hour with you after tea.
> Violet: Yes, but it was an hour *every day*.
> Isobel: [momentarily lost for words] I see, yes. How tiring![44]

Let's face it, women love change—at least some kinds of it: rearranging furniture, buying clothes, a change of scenery to break up the mundane. Entire industries are built up around the expectation that we want change: new makeup, plastic changes to our chins, lifts to our wrinkles, weight loss, new shoes. "New and Improved" is a cornerstone of marketing for a reason. Motherhood, however, is much more of a marathon than a sprint. Yes, there are different stages to it, but as the dowager countess knows well, it does have an on-and-on-ness about it that is opposed to new and improved.

In his famous aria "La donna è mobile," from the opera *Rigoletto*, Giuseppe Verdi captured this feminine vice perfectly. A translation of the Italian lyrics says: "Woman is flighty / Like a feather in the wind / She changes her voice and her mind."[45]

When we are young, we can be flighty with seemingly no consequences. It seems fun to keep people—particularly members of the opposite sex—guessing.

Motherhood, on the other hand, can rein in this shallow excess. Time takes on new meaning as the demands of a baby's schedule and the needs of growing children. If we allow our flighty or fickle nature to rule our homes, it won't be long before we realize that things aren't going very well—that our children are always fussy because their needs aren't met, that our homes lack order and beauty, and that catering to our whims never seems to help the situation.

Individualism

Angela had been married seven years. Her husband had made it clear during that time that he really wanted to have children. "I feel like getting something new," Angela told her hopeful husband one afternoon.

"Honey," he replied, "that feeling is your biological clock telling you it is time to have a baby. You are in your mid-thirties. You don't have much time left."

"Hmmm," she said. "I was thinking more along the lines of a new cat or a bird."

Angela is not alone. Like many women, deep down she is afraid of what would happen to the woman she knows herself to be if she were faced with caring, day in and day out, for a baby. And she is afraid because she has seen the hard work that goes into being a mother. Motherhood is not for the faint of heart.

Women like Angela are common in our world today: afraid of having a child, afraid of how it will change their lives, afraid of the unknown. Our culture is saturated with the ideology of the individual. Individualism is slightly different than simple vanity because a woman can adopt the ideology without even being aware that it is a vice. Her energies may be directed at very good and wholesome goals. Nonetheless, the imprint is still strongly there upon most of us. We are used to having what we want, when we want it, how we want it. All of these comfortable realities come to a screeching halt once we have children. For the woman used to operating as a monad, the reality of doing everything for a helpless child can be daunting. "What happened to me?" even the most prepared new mother may ask.

The transition to motherhood is a hard one, particularly for women who are used to doing "big" things in a career. There are no raises, no bonuses, no promotions, usually not even many acknowledgments of a job well done—even though it is the toughest job you've ever had.

I remember shortly after I found out that I was pregnant with my first child, I went to help my sister with her two small children when she delivered her third. Up to that point, I had been living in Italy and before that Washington, D.C., making snap decisions about my day-to-day life: *Where will I go for lunch today? Should I go shopping?* Planning in advance, other than flights or haircuts, just wasn't something I did much of. And unless I was joining other people for a meal, I didn't really need to consult the schedules of others. Then I went to my sister's house. I was amazed at how much work it was to keep after two children. "You have to get every meal for them, *every day!*" I said to myself. "Sheesh. This is a lot of work." I laughed about it with a friend, a mother of three, and she assured me that it happens gradually enough that it isn't nearly as difficult as taking over the care of two older children. I was still not convinced.

And then my own child arrived. I remember feeling nostalgic for my old life: "I have to take this baby carrier everywhere I go now? This is going to be rough." Don't get me wrong—I was thrilled to have this precious child and loved everything about her, but that transition to being a mother was a tough one after the many years when it had just been me. Gone were the snap decisions in my life. All those familiar realities changed. Suddenly her schedule and needs trumped everything. Before long every day presented a new "little death" to my own will when I couldn't finish even the smallest of projects because of the needs of my babies.

Pope Francis has talked about how mothers heal the wound of individualism: "Mothers are the strongest antidote to the spread of egotistical individualism." Individual, the pope explained, "means 'that it cannot be divided.' Mothers, instead, 'divide themselves,' from the moment they host a child to give him to the world and make him grow."[46] Recalling his own mother, the Holy Father said:

> A mother always has problems with her children, always has work. I remember at home—we were five children—and while one did one thing, another thought of doing another, and our poor mother went from one to the other, but she was happy. She gave us so much.[47]

The pope's mother, like other mothers who live the gracious spirit, was both harried and happy.

Impatience

Shannon knew she was impatient going into motherhood. But as the challenges of caring for little ones and balancing all her responsibilities wore on, she found herself with a shorter and shorter fuse and lashing out more at her children than she really wanted. And then one day, it happened: Her five-year-old son yelled at his little sister *exactly* like Shannon yelled at him. Hearing her own harsh tone in her son's voice made her realize something had to change.

Impatience is a vice exacerbated by our individualism. We just aren't taught extended patience for much of anything. There are few examples in life, however, that demand more patience than dealing with children, especially when you get more than one or two together.

While practice had a significant effect on my own struggles to be patient, a major breakthrough came for me through the example of a friend. Jane was a mother of two who had worked as a mover and shaker in New York before having children. Knowing her background as a city girl, I never dreamed that she would have a lamblike disposition when it came to children. It was fascinating to watch Jane transformed by a small child. She would get down to his level, smile, speak in hushed tones, and just be present for this little person, as if to say, "You are the only thing that matters right now, and you have every ounce of my attention." Now, of course, Jane's attitude isn't something I can use all the time, but I was astounded to see how her gentle, quiet way not only helped engage the child, but was a real example to me of how to get through my own petty irritations and frustrations.

Patience also needs perseverance. These might be the hallmark habits any mother must acquire to make it through the day. There is nothing like the endurance needed to get everything done. My own motto for daily life has become: "Keep moving." If I stop for too long, I may not get up again.

There is, however, no surer way than motherhood to learn to be patient with the needs of others or to persevere in difficult circumstances. I recently tried to surrender; the challenges of the day and the night before were just too much for me to bear after another night of only a couple of hours of sleep. I wanted to wave the white flag, to surrender. And then I realized I didn't have the luxury of having someone to surrender to (sigh). After asking our Lord for help and offering my struggles back to him, I had to just keep moving until some relief was in sight from my husband. When we think, however, that we have hit the edge of our capacity, there is usually more in reserve. Practice, perspective, and patience in the face of necessity can go a long way.

One exuberant new mother recently said to me: "I'm amazed at how hard it is to be selfish now!" And she is right—motherhood offers the most gentle correction to our most prideful tendencies.

Questions for Reflection

1. In what ways are you your own worst enemy when it comes to raising your children?

2. How do you think your own life struggles could be diminished through an awareness of your own pride?

3. Can you see how growth in these virtues helps in other areas of your life?

SEVEN

Organizing Our Stuff

Let us treasure up in our soul some of those things
which are permanent . . . , not of those which
will forsake us and be destroyed, and which
only tickle our senses for a little while . . .

—St. Gregory of Nazianzen[48]

As women, most of us have a difficult relationship with stuff—it is so easy for us to overvalue some stuff, while undervaluing other stuff. Food? Can't get enough of that stuff. Money? Bring it on. More clothes? Sure. Another kid? Whoa. Wait a minute. Not so fast. Then I might not have enough of the other stuff.

In addition to our battle with vanity, Edith Stein astutely observed our twisted relationship to *things.* Speaking mainly about how women view children as "property for their own purposes," Stein was able to pinpoint why it is so difficult for so many of us to be open to the idea of more children. She explains that based upon our feminine nature, when it is twisted toward vice, a woman can easily consider "others as her property or as means for her own purposes."[49] Women can "develop an unhealthy possession of their children, seen in a dominating will rather than a joyful service."[50] To this could also be added a new way of treating children as possessions: neglect. The contraception/abortion mentality society has lived with for more than half a century (and well after Stein was writing) has made parenting an option, in which children could exist or not exist. This choice allows women (and men) to view their roles in a much more laissez-faire light; a child then becomes to mothers, (and fathers) as something to add to life—an object—as long as he or she doesn't interfere with it too much. (Naturally, there are other reasons couples choose not to have more children that don't violate Catholic teaching, but this is unfortunately one of them in our materialistic culture.)

The response to all of these is joyful service to the unrepeatable souls in our care. A woman "must consider others as gifts entrusted to her, and she can only do so when she also sees them as God's creatures towards whom she has a holy duty to fulfill."[51] The more we are open to sacrificing our own immediate needs, the greater the love we feel and the more joy we experience. It is a simple formula, really—but not one that can be seen easily from the outside. Like Pope St. John Paul II said, we find ourselves only in giving ourselves away.

Control Freak

The "dominating will" discussed by Stein is another vice women can easily fall into when it comes to possessions. One manifestation of this is the control freak. We have all encountered her, and many of us have been her at times (ahem). There is nothing like being a mother to help us abandon any illusions we may have had that we can control very much. Children have a way of unhinging that idea very quickly, while giving us the opportunity to place in the hands of God all that we love in all those awkward, tiresome, frustrating moments throughout the day.

"I am never doing that when I have a baby." How many of us have said that and then when we have a child, sure enough, whatever "that" was, we are doing it. My friend Alex was adamant that she would never let her daughter use a pacifier. One night she caved. Eventually her daughter could not be pacified by just one, but needed three of them: one for her mouth and one for each hand to hold when she went to sleep.

The art of motherhood humbles us in so many ways, but instances like these, in which we throw out whatever sort of mom's code we had before we were moms, is the best inoculation against being uncharitable to others—particularly other moms, those we naturally feel inclined to compare ourselves with. The "I would never do that" scenarios dissolve once we find ourselves doing exactly what we vowed we would never do.

Laura had been a neat freak all her life. Every pillow, sheet, towel, and dish had to be in its place. And then she had children. Suddenly, making sure that the faucet was perfectly lined up with the center of the sink was no longer a priority. How quickly she realized that she simply didn't have time to keep her house as immaculate as it had been, while also seeing that it just wasn't that important.

The vice of trying to control situations is one that most of us shed simply through the natural circumstances of motherhood. The virtues, of course, are abandonment to God's will in our life, trust, and hope. We don't know everything, we can't anticipate every situation, and good doses of just going with the flow help temper the control freak in all of us. We have to learn to trust that God is in control of our lives and no amount of trying to control a situation will change that. This abandonment is also the key to a free, childlike (not childish) spirit. This was the spirit Mamoo possessed at age eighty. It gave her soul the freedom to laugh at herself and live joyfully in the grace of the moment.

Avarice and Gluttony

Our culture, unfortunately, is awash in stuff. We live in the wealthiest society known to man. It is easy to find delight, consolation, and distraction in shopping and eating. However, satiating our every need and whimsical desire is about the worst thing for anyone—particularly for women. With all these distractions, it is easy to rely too much upon the emotions that carry us away to the next sale or the all-you-can-eat buffet, and then try to hide our overspending from our husbands or go on a crash diet to make up for our intemperance. Credit card debt and the diet industry are the real barometers of our spiritual health.

Like the other vices, avarice and gluttony can be tempered through motherhood. For starters, caring for children and a family can strain the resources of any budget, depending on one's spending habits. There is usually little room for that new pair of shoes, frequent dinners out, or exciting travel, particularly once issues of saving for college, private school, or extra-curricular activities come into play.

But money is not the only thing women need to learn to be frugal with—there is also time. Time might even be more of a restricted commodity than money in the early years with children. Gone are the hours of leisure time for sipping coffee in a trendy coffee shop, long chats with friends, going to movies, or even just reading a good book. There never seem to be enough hours in the day to get everything on your list done.

Temperance, which is basically the practice of working within your means—whether it be time or money—comes into play when a woman has to look out for more than just her own life. It has the added bonus of helping us to make good decisions about dealing with food. In many ways, food is just like money—if I overspend here, I pay for it somewhere. Having large swaths of time to go to the gym to make up for the four doughnuts I ate this morning because I was bored just isn't going to happen. We also know that others are actually depending on us, so our health becomes even more import-ant than when it was just about getting ready for swimsuit weather. When we practice the virtue of temperance and be-come used to trimming our desires in one area, it is easier to trim them in others. The virtues work together that way.

Additionally, this shaving down of stuff—be it free time or money—through motherhood has a way of making us ap-preciate the importance of the spiritual realities. The weight of our love for our children and our deep desire to see their well-being brings into focus not only the love God has for us, but the realization that we let things unnecessarily get in the way of loving him in return.

The Noonday Devil, or Sloth

For many years, Rebecca found herself discouraged in prayer, wondering if her efforts actually did anything. Yes, she thought prayers had been answered, but what endured was this discouraging nagging feeling that her prayers didn't amount to much. She was suffering from the vice of sloth.

Sloth is a word rarely heard these days—it conjures up images of a smelly teenage boy's room, complete with the idle teen zoned out on some screen—but women, slothful? No. Well, unfortunately, our understanding of it doesn't quite capture the ancient and medieval usage of the term. Distraction, desire for novelty, boredom, dissipated focus, and discouragement are the signs of the vice of sloth. It is that drive that says, "I'm bored with this. Let's move on." It can be called the "noonday devil" because fourth- and fifth-century monks living in the desert reported a certain type of malaise that would set into their spirits around noon, when the sun was at its highest. They would find any excuse to leave what they were there to do: prayer and meditation.

One of the sixth-century Desert Fathers of the Church offered this advice to those struggling to stay the course of their vocation: Imagine you are in a dark tunnel. To find your way, you must stay close to the wall—what you know. Do what you always do and just persevere until you find the other side. Or, as he put it more simply for his audience, "If you need to eat: eat. If you need to sleep: sleep. But don't leave your cell."[52] Stay the course. Or as Winston Churchill said: "If you are going through hell, keep going."[53] The best way to deal with sloth is truly perseverance, while being ever mindful that you are called to serve others with a gentle spirit. As a mother, even if your mind turns to your own petty concerns of boredom, fatigue, or frustration, there is always something else to concern yourself with. The pace and demands of motherhood offer the grace to pull us out of our own heads and pour more of ourselves into those around us who need the love of a mother.

In chapters two and three, we explored the feminine vocation. Part of that call includes what is at the heart of every woman (barring damage or distorting vice): the desire for wholeness within herself and the ability to give of her wealth to improve the lives of others. The feminine vices, as we have just seen, render that desire impotent because with selfishness and self-absorption, a woman simply cannot get beyond herself. No matter how she tries, happiness will *always* remain elusive because it is in the giving of herself, to repeat the quote from Pope John Paul II, that she finds herself and her bliss.

Questions for Reflection

1. Are there areas in your life or society at large where you can see stuff placed above life?

2. What ways can you reorder your life so that spiritual and human values are honored more than material things?

3. Is there a way that living these virtues learned in motherhood can be helpful in other areas of your life?

EIGHT

Bridling Our Emotions

There is no sin nor wrong that gives man such a
foretaste of Hell in this life as anger and impatience.

—St. Catherine of Siena[54]

We live in a very emotional world. In many ways, what we feel in our hearts has come to dominate what we know in our heads. On an average day, it is easy to experience the emotional whiplash of social media. As we scroll through Facebook, we may feel elation, frustration, sadness, anger, and joy all within seconds. And as every journalist can tell you, appealing to an emotional response, particularly anger, outrage, shock, or sorrow, sells papers. Our culture is awash in what is called in rhetoric "pathos," or an appeal to the emotions. Even when our minds can easily trump the emotions with a logical argument, somehow the emotions, which have been given free rein over our souls, win.

Unfortunately, the emotions get less attention than they should when it comes to our moral life. Confessors and husbands are reluctant to talk about them. "What do you mean, I'm too emotional?" is the expected response, which confirms the diagnosis but does not solve the problem. There are certainly resources for dealing with our emotions, particularly anger and sadness—but it is a topic that we tend to shy away from and chalk up to our temperament or hormones. Of course, those are both strong forces in a woman's life, but we aren't doing ourselves any favors by not talking about them within the context of virtues and vices. Many negative emotions can be reined in.

The emotions, when not tended to, can lead to a dizzying array of difficulties. Spiritual directors, particularly those trained in the tools of discernment according to St. Ignatius, make it clear that the emotions are an easy way for the devil to deceive us by tempting us through a negative emotion. Strong flashes of anger, indignation, fear, or even lingering feelings of apathy can be red flags. While this is not the place to go deeper into this discussion, the best way to protect ourselves against both the devil and becoming enslaved to our emotions is by recognizing that emotions can be curtailed.[55]

Edith Stein again offers many insights into how the emotions take over our reasoning faculty, or intellect.

> Intellect is the light which illuminates its path, and without this light, emotion changes back and forth. In fact, if emotions prevail over the intellect, it is able to obscure the light and distort the picture of the entire world. . . . Emotional stirrings need the control of reason and the direction of the will."[56]

Stein makes clear that it is our intellect that must rule our emotions for us to see reality clearly. Unfortunately, in our secular culture, many people mistake having strong emotions on a given topic for actually thinking about the issue.

While both men and women need to develop their minds, women's propensity for the emotional life can be dangerous. "Where discipline of mind and will are lacking, emotional life becomes a compulsion without secure direction," Stein explains. "And because it always needs some stimulation for its activity, it becomes addicted to sensuality,"[57] without being guided by the mind and will. Stein continues by explaining that because of the union of body and soul, the overly emotional and sensual woman will not grow in spirituality, but will remain stuck in the material.

In addition to physical sensuality, often women fall in love with the emotions associated with love. I recall hearing one woman say, "I'm in love with being in love." She was talking about those early feelings a couple experiences in the bloom of a new relationship. Our divorce courts are filled with people who didn't know how hard marriage could be, confusing those early-bloom feelings with true and abiding love. These emotions act like training wheels for a relationship, getting a couple started and setting them apart from the wider community, but then the relationship must either move on to the deeper realities of self-gift or fall apart.[58]

Motherhood, more than most other types of love, quickly acclimates us to what true love is: *an act of the will, not simply a feeling.* What mother has warm feelings about getting up to soothe a crying baby in the middle of the night? Or battling a willful toddler? Or helping a child with homework after a long day? These are acts of love that generally engage our will, not our affections. Once we are used to *loving* others *through our will* instead of being motivated by a strong emotion that pleases us, it becomes much easier to love others—our husbands, parents, siblings, strangers, and particularly God—with this same kind of love. Motherhood awakens the will. St. John of the Cross and other saints have made clear that we are judged by our love—in terms of acts of the will—instead of simply a fleeting *feeling*.

Emotions, of course, are not all bad. They just need to be informed by the intellect and the will. We cannot act upon every whim and fancy. As Stein explains, "It is thereby possible for the emotional responses themselves to be judged as being 'right' or 'wrong,' or 'inappropriate.' It is a matter of awakening joyful emotion for authentic beauty and goodness and disgust for that which is base and vulgar."[59] When we grow spiritually and grow in virtue, the reality of the good, true, and beautiful becomes more evident to us, while we simultaneously become more horrified at that which is ugly, crass, and vile.

For moms and expectant moms, the day is riddled with events that could set even the calmest woman on edge, but these emotions need to be redirected. How many of us live with deep anger, frustration, irritation, or envy? These are all relatively easy to hide when we live on our own—but add a few children and they become volcanic. We simply have to find a way to deal with them in a healthy manner—by rooting them out at the source (sometimes with pastoral or professional help) or finding a healthy way to channel them. The best way, of course, is to offer them back to Christ—to let him transform them into something beautiful. Our will needs to become stronger than our emotions, and it can happen when we know where to direct them, or whom to give them to. One priest likened the emotions to a dog—a wild one will be a terror, while a tame one is a quiet comfort and companion. Battling our emotions daily opens the door to freeing ourselves and our families from their tyranny, rather than just hiding them in a closet.

So what is the proper response to all of these overgrown emotional vices? A virtue that I admit I knew very little about as I began to write this book: meekness. Yes, meekness. Meekness is not what you think—it doesn't mean being a spineless milquetoast or a coward, but quite the contrary. It is the most misunderstood of the virtues. There is, in fact, nothing weak about being meek. It is the woman of unique strength who, although she is clearly aware of adverse realities around her, is able to direct her emotions to an appropriate response in a difficult situation.

Let me give you an example of what I mean. Stella spent years traveling for work when she was single, and because she flew so much, she became a very impatient traveler, always expecting the best. Several years after she and her husband decided she would stay home with their children, she traveled with her kids to visit her parents. Stripped of her privileged travel status, she knew she could no long expect special perks. Little, however, prepared her for how poorly she was treated on one leg of her flight. After overhearing the steward report that there were going to be VIPs on the plane, Stella and her children were mysteriously moved from row 6 to row 19. And then they were moved again, this time to the very last row of the plane, row 24. Focused on trying to be meek, Stella didn't respond to the situation as perhaps she would have five years earlier. She knew she had been bumped back because everyone was concerned that her children would disturb the VIPs, but rather than exploding, she simply tried to make the best of it.

Meekness, then, is the embodiment of deep interior strength and authentic mastery over our emotions. It is also a sign of profound faith, in which it is clear that the woman knows that everything that happens in her life is a part of God's providence. It happens in our lives because it is either positively willed by God (the good) or allowed by him (the evils, bad things, trials, sufferings, struggles, etc.) for a greater good, often to help us grow ever closer to him, to rely more on him.

Over the past seven years, I have spent nearly every Sunday in the cry room at one church or another. I had no idea that doing so would be such a classroom of meekness. The cry room, or as I lovingly refer to it, the "penalty box," comes with a cost. I think of it as purgatory. The thought of putting together in a very small, usually stuffy and hot room the most sleep-deprived, hormonal set of adults in the parish and then adding scads of children of varying dispositions, levels of crankiness, eating habits, and disciplinary codes seems like a recipe for disaster.

As my husband can attest, for the first few years I would come out of Mass fuming, feeling like I needed to head from the penalty box to the confessional box. In retrospect much of it was because of the harsh transition from being in the front row of the church with undivided attention to being in a box in the back of the church with every conceivable distraction. *How many more years do I have to do this?* was my constant thought back then. Additionally, there was the steep motherhood curve and learning about different parenting approaches.

Internally I kept something of a Mass clock in my mind: "Okay, we made it through the homily. Let's see if we can get through the Eucharistic prayer." The end of every Mass felt like a triumph of the spirit to have completed my Sunday obligation without a major meltdown (mine or the child's).

What I learned from the intense reality of the cry room is that I can't control the behavior of anyone except my child (sometimes) and myself, particularly my own internal disposition. Getting angry and frustrated with the chaos and irreverence around me wasn't leading me any closer to God. But I also began to see how this new ability to contain my emotions was spilling into other areas of my life and allowing me to let go of many of the emotional struggles I had previously held on to.

Meekness also provides an open place within the soul of a woman to hear God's voice, to become docile to his will. The emotions, without a positive place to put them, can lock us up in our own thoughts, wants, and fixations. Only the clear flow of grace that comes from the practice of meekness can purify our intentions, giving our souls the space to let God do what he must to further transform us.

Questions for Reflection

1. What emotions do you struggle with the most?

2. How do you think your relationships would be improved if you could better deal with those areas that you struggle with?

3. Why is the effort to strengthen your will important in battling the emotions?

NINE

Anxiety and the Lost Art of Contemplation

By the anxieties and worries of this life Satan tries to
dull man's heart and make a dwelling for himself there.

—St. Francis of Assisi[60]

Women worry. We worry like it is our job. We are professional worriers. But, surprisingly, worrying is not a virtue.
While on some level it feels like worry and anxiety happen to
us and we must passively accept them, worry is actually a vice
that we can control. Yes, unfortunately, sometimes anxiety has
more to do with hormones, stress, or other emotional wounds,
but in general we are not helpless in the fight against it.

Many women I know cast their thoughts out to some place
in the future, and like waves, the worries of what could happen between now and that given point roll into the current
moment. There is nothing like a midnight feeding or insom-
nia in the wee hours of the night to make the waves of concern
get larger, scarier, and more real. Other women imagine the
worst and then see it as some sort of premonition, while still
others turn their thoughts to the past and worry about how
they ought to have done things differently. Nagging thoughts,
such as *If only I hadn't done that* or *Why did I say that?* consume
our souls with regret, shame, embarrassment, or anger—or all

of the above. There is not, however, a lot of discussion about how to deal with anxiety, unless, of course, you are interested in getting on some kind of medication for it. I suspect many of women's worries come from an unconscious belief that worrying will somehow keep bad things at bay—that if we think it could happen, it won't. It is always the unexpected that happens, right? Therefore, by thinking of something before it happens, we must be somehow controlling the situation. Or if we worry about something in advance, perhaps we'll be better prepared to deal with it.

So what do we do about worry?

I've often wondered about this line in Scripture: "And Mary pondered these things in her heart" (Luke 2:19). What was Mary pondering, and why was she doing it? Wasn't she busy worrying like every other woman? And what about Simeon's prophecy that her heart would be pierced by a sword? Didn't that keep her up at night? Yet Luke and the other Evangelists make no mention of Mary worrying. There is no passage like "Mary tossed and turned all night worrying" or "Mary furrowed her brow and tried to hide her fretting about the future." And why didn't Mary worry? Because she trusted God and humbly submitted herself to everything in his divine providence. Most of us, however, need a bit more help because of our own imperfections.

Yes, women clearly have a propensity to worry. But we also have a gift for contemplation; we marinate ideas in our minds and hearts. Scripture makes it clear that Mary, through pondering—or, as some translations say, treasuring—contemplated elements of Christ's life and divinity. She ruminated over ideas, memories, miracles, wonders, and perhaps sorrows, much like we are instructed to do while praying the Rosary.

Could it be that worry is the sinful or broken side of the contemplation spectrum, revealing our lack of trust and fallen nature? Perhaps instead we are called to contemplate the mystery of God, the wonder of our lives, the beauty of our children, while simultaneously showing our profound trust in a Father who loves us. By worrying, we take the good of contemplation and turn it into anxiety through our lack of trust in God's providence.

Many of us don't really know that we can and should combat these worries, because they have become so second nature. The uselessness of worry is made clear in Scripture: "Can any of you by worrying add a single moment to your life-span?" (Matthew 6:27). St. Bernard spoke of "carrying your own weather," meaning, don't let the darkness around you steal your peace and joy. Somewhere I picked up the idea of "guarding your peace" as the best defense against anxiety. The idea of guarding it seems important, because it takes real work to protect our interior emotional life, which can be so swiftly unhinged.

I have four children. Each pregnancy has had its own set of irrational worries. The first child ushered in major concerns about the garbage disposal. I can't tell you why, but I had to have everyone out of the kitchen before I could turn it on. Thankfully, that hormone-induced concern has passed. When I was pregnant with my third child, I was fixated on the baby's health. I was nearing age thirty-nine and had passed that magic number when the chances of something going wrong with the pregnancy jump from negligible to noticeable. My worries were certainly fed by the increased amount of testing, genetic counseling, and prenatal care the industry throws at us old ladies (and our "geriatric" wombs, as they are called). And while on one hand, any child God gave to me would have been a blessing, I was consumed with anxiety about this one. It was a great relief when the ultrasound showed a healthy baby boy, with no missing limbs, no altered chromosomes, and no major health concerns. Later that afternoon, as I was lying down for a nap, I was thanking God for his mercy and generosity. Then it was as if a gentle voice spoke to my heart:

"I am not in your worries."

"You are not in my worries?" I asked.

"No."

"So, all my worries are really my own doing?"

"Yes."

"So, by worrying, I'm not really controlling the universe, or my own little corner of it."

"No."

"So, I really don't have to worry?"

"No."

I suddenly felt a deep sense of relief and peace. Of course, my next thought was to worry that I might forget not to worry. Old habits die hard. But as with any habit, time, patience, and practice would help correct my fault.

Once I started to let go of my anxiety in earnest (granted, there have been many stumbles along the way) I was amazed at the fruit I saw in other areas of my life. Those pendulum swings of emotion that tinged my every thought with fear or anxiety were gone. I had a lot more patience because my own emotions weren't constantly exhausting me.

One difficult reality that arises when letting go of worry is our tendency to try to fill the void. What else can I think about? As women, we do have a great potential for contemplation—yes, in the Rosary, but we also contemplate other spiritual things. Contemplation or pondering, as it is described in Scripture, is like adding oxygen to a fire, the fire of our faith and our love of God. It can also serve as a rudder in the midst of storms.

In the face of adversity, Fiona was given a lesson in contemplation. She had recently lost her beloved grandmother, and her best friend was moving away. These women had been anchors in her life. The familiar relationships she had previously relied upon were no longer there to offer support. Certainly she had great memories, but everything else felt different. Even the town she lived in felt bigger because the places where her loved ones had lived now felt empty and cold. When she went to prayer, she tried to make sense of what her new life was going to look like without these important women supporting her. Everything had changed.

And yet, in this storm of emotions, Fiona found herself doing something unusual. She found that the only place her thoughts could go where she wouldn't have to adjust to change was in contemplating God. He alone was the only thing she could go to that was a constant. So when she found herself getting anxious about something, she felt prompted to consider his many constant and enduring attributes: goodness, eternal life, steadfast love, and enormity. Even the simple Scripture verse "Be still and know that I am God" (Psalm 46:11) was enough to allow Fiona to refocus. Here, in these thoughts and prayers—in this contemplation—she found something solid to rest upon again.

Fiona found the simple art of contemplation. Nothing fancy, just a place to rest her mind, to marinate ideas about God. She discovered the art of what St. Teresa of Avila taught: that contemplation is simply a friendly conversation with God. She learned to take his promptings, hold them close to her heart, and internalize them. It is shockingly similar to worrying, yet its fruit is dramatically different: freeing, grounding, ordering, and calming, while reminding us that we are not alone and are loved.

The Christian life is about embracing our crosses and surrendering our lives to God's providence. The life of any woman is full of twists and turns, different seasons that change dramatically. Through Mary's example of pondering, we know we don't have to go out to meet our troubles. As I have started telling my children, we only have the grace for the present moment. When the future arrives, the grace we need for whatever happens will be ready for us. In the meantime, we will be much more peaceful and joyful if we give up worrying and try to contemplate God in his goodness as a true foretaste of what is to come in eternal life. There is nothing so freeing as abandoning our every word, deed, and thought to the one who created us. Perhaps St. Teresa of Avila said it best:

Let nothing disturb you,
Let nothing frighten you,
All things are passing:
God never changes.
Patience obtains all things
Whoever has God lacks nothing:
God alone suffices.[61]

And when we feel ourselves backsliding into anxiety, we simply need to listen for the still, small voice. God will whisper: "Don't worry. I am here. Ponder me."

Questions for Reflection

1. If you struggle with anxiety, what kinds of worries are the most common for you?

2. How can trust and abandonment to God relieve these particular concerns?

3. Are there certain Bible passages or scenes from Scripture that you can imagine turning to when anxiety sets in?

The Wealth of Wisdom

Who can find a woman of worth? Far
beyond jewels is her value.

—Proverbs 51:10

While on vacation in Portland, Oregon, my family and I went out for an evening stroll for ice cream in the trendiest pocket of town. Coming toward us were two women covered in tattoos and piercings, dressed in thrift-store Goth. As we crossed paths, we overheard one of them say: "I don't know, perhaps something is wrong with my decision-making process?" It was such a fitting line to hear from someone who appeared to be in need of a lot of love and guidance. And she was probably right. Years of being told—because it is a cultural mantra—"Do whatever you want" have created a deep viciousness that clouds the mind. It is difficult to see with any clarity when vice has taken over (which is one reason why common sense isn't very common anymore).

In fact, it is entirely possible to live with a feeling that you are doing something very good and still be doing something objectively awful. Gabby was just such a soul. In college she wanted to apply her skills in a way that would help promote her political interests. Being pro-choice, she volunteered to be an escort at the local Planned Parenthood. Flushed with excitement about doing something really grassroots, Gabby went to work. It didn't take long for her to get it. The other escorts were bitter, coarse, rude, and triumphalist in their opposition to the pro-life protesters. Meanwhile, the character of the folks on the other side of the sidewalk was one of peace, calm, and charity—particularly in the face of such opposition. After two months she called it quits. The disparity between her convictions and the reality on the sidewalk was just too great. And yet, she had been so convinced that she was on the right side of the argument. What the Desert Fathers have explained is that true charity leads to meekness, while activism only leads to bitterness. We can see the difference through the fruits of our actions.

There is an interesting element of the virtues that I haven't touched upon yet: The virtues work together, they grow together, and they can be pulled down by the weakest link. Think of an old paint can—if you just pop one side, the lid may not budge, but steady effort around the whole lid will eventually pry open the can. This is also why the virtues are difficult to discuss and distill into tight definitions, because of their connectedness. So if you are excelling in a certain area of the virtues, the strength of a great vice can pull everything back down to viciousness. It's like a sweater that is in the process of being knitted: The virtues knit, the vices unknit, but the sweater can't be finished until the knitting is finished and the unknitting ends.

The fruit of all the knitting, when the virtues are working together, is prudence and wisdom. These are the insights, judgments, and right decisions that can be made or discovered when we can see things as they are without the plank in our eye distorting our vision. St. Thomas Aquinas said, "Wisdom, which is a gift, is not the cause but the effect of charity,"[62] meaning God gives us wisdom as a crowning gift when we exercise the virtues, in particular the virtue of charity, or the love of neighbor.

Betsy is the busy mother of five. Early in her marriage, she and her husband had worked together on international projects. When she started having children, she scaled back her work, while her husband became busier and more successful with the work they had previously done together. She shared in his joy at the success the early seeds of their work together had borne, but each new child's arrival confirmed all the more that she just needed to be home with them, despite the temptation to share directly in her husband's success. Eventually, her husband was approached with a movie contract, which would take his work to a whole new level professionally and help them financially. However, fame and fortune were going to come at a cost—more travel, more time apart, more stress on their family. Despite her husband's excitement at the offer, Betsy was able to persuade him that the movie deal was not in the best interest of their family. Betsy knew that she couldn't sacrifice the peace and balance of their family life, which had to be a priority if they were going to raise their children to be saints. Most of us wouldn't be able to pass up what Betsy did—we would find some way to justify it: "Think of all the good things we could do with the money." And yet, that's usually how wisdom looks—it isn't obvious to the world, but it is to the wise woman.

Share Our Strength

Edith Stein makes it clear that when we are living as hand-maids of the Lord, following his will and growing into whole persons, there will be signal changes in our lives. For starters, there will be subtle but perceptible changes in reverence, gentleness, and goodness. A woman's thirst to know more of God will deepen. She will also come to recognize that every gift she has been given is meant to be shared with others in generosity and love. She will look for new opportunities to make sacrifices for others or to help those in need. And she will see that those who need the most love are the hardest to love.

No matter what the specific vocation of a woman, in order to carry it out properly, Stein ascribes these essential virtues:

> The soul of woman must therefore be *expansive* and open to all human beings; it must be *quiet* so that no small flame will be extinguished by stormy winds; *warm* so as not to benumb fragile buds; *clear,* so that no vermin will settle in dark corners and recesses; *self-contained,* so that no invasions from without can imperil the inner life; *empty of itself* and also of its body, so that the entire person is readily at the disposal of every call.[63]

It is this sort of woman whom Pope St. John Paul II called "the perfect woman":

> In every age and in every country we find many "perfect" women (cf. *Prov.* 31:10) who, despite persecution, diffi-

culties and discrimination, have shared in the Church's mission. . . . The witness and the achievements of Christian women have had a significant impact on the life of the Church as well as of society. Even in the face of serious social discrimination, holy women have acted "freely," strengthened by their union with Christ. Such union and freedom rooted in God explain, for example, the great work of Saint Catherine of Siena in the life of the Church, and the work of Saint Teresa of Jesus in the monastic life.[64]

John Paul goes on to mention many other perfect women, among them Monica, the mother of Augustine; Jadwiga of Cracow; Bridget of Sweden; Joan of Arc; Rose of Lima; and Elizabeth Ann Seton. It is hard to imagine a more varied group of women in terms of background, experience, vocation, etc., and yet they are all bound by their holiness and faithfulness to our Lord's call.

And so it is for any woman who answers God's call. Stein adds that "because streams of living water flow from all those who live in God's hand, they exert a mysterious magnetic appeal on thirsty souls."[65] The wise woman will become a pillar that others will try to fasten themselves to as something solid and a source of strength, insight, and guidance. Or to use another metaphor from Stein, these women become energized spores that go out into the community and pass their goodness on to those in their path. Pope John Paul II said something similar: "Thus the 'perfect woman' (cf. Proverbs 31:10) becomes an irreplaceable support and source of spiritual strength for other people, who perceive the great energies of her spirit."[66]

Every vice discussed in the previous pages takes away a mother's strength, her trustworthiness, her very ability to be the anchor of the family, holding it together and keeping the whole ship from capsizing in the storms of life. Without Mama, things can go terribly wrong. And without a strong, true, trusted, constant mother, there is no telling where the members of the ship might end up. This is not to devalue in any way the importance of fathers—but there is something supremely important and unique about a mother's love, which at its core provides nurturing, safety, and affection that is all but impossible to find elsewhere.

Questions for Reflection

1. Think of other examples of wise women. Are there common patterns in their decisions or choice of actions?

2. What qualities do you think the "perfect woman" Pope John Paul II spoke of had?

3. Do you think these qualities are the same for every culture and age? If not, what qualities would a "perfect woman" of our own age need?

ELEVEN

Survival Strategies—When Wit's End Is a Real Place

Let us throw ourselves into the ocean of His goodness, where every failing will be canceled and anxiety turned into love.

—St. Paul of the Cross[67]

"These are the symptoms to look for, and if they appear, you need to go to the hospital immediately," my perinatologist told me gravely as he gave me an update on the life-threatening condition I had during my last pregnancy. "And you need to stay off your feet." Seeing the strain on my face, he said gently, "Do I need to talk to your husband to get some help for you?" With three small children and another on the way, putting my feet up to rest didn't seem to be much of an option.

There are times when every mother would like to surrender because she is at her wit's end, only to quickly realize that there is no one to surrender to. It seems like a luxury to be able to say, "Can you take over? I just need a break to go hide." Sometimes, there is no grandmother or aunt to call, no friend nearby to help, no fairy godmother to come to the rescue.

While there are many reasons why motherhood can feel so difficult, one of the most overlooked is the fallout from the 1960s sexual revolution that seems to have no end in sight. I've often thought that a woman should be given an extra arm with the arrival of a new child. Historically there were plenty of extra hands around to help out a struggling mother. Neighborhoods brimming with families and small children were common-place, along with an abundance of local aunts, grandparents, and cousins to call upon when necessary. Today, rather than there being a friendly family next door, most houses are empty as everyone heads to work, school, or daycare. And instead of bringing over a meal or offering to watch older children, those who could help frequently serve up a heaping of incredulity and even condescension that anyone would willingly have more than two children. "You got yourself into this mess" is often the prevailing attitude in our radically individualistic culture. As a result, it can take a lot of work and time to actually create a net-work of friends to count on when needs arise. Even having an-other baby can feel like an advanced course in management to make sure all the bases are covered while you are at the hospital.

Most mothers can tell you of a time or two when they re-ally just didn't know how they were going to make it through the day. Sometimes, they will say, there were entire seasons when they felt like a dried leaf that could crumple into a thou-sand pieces with the slightest squeeze. It is then that moms need mothering. They need comfort, relief, joy, delight, grat-itude, and tears from the balm of maternal touch. And yes, while husbands can be a great consolation, often they are just as stressed out and tired as you are. It's important to have some idea of where to look when you don't know where else to turn.

As discussed in previous chapters, part of the struggle to grow in virtue involves being pushed beyond your limits.

These situations too can be instructive for those of us with an independent, "I can do it all myself" mentality. God has not made us to be an island, but formed us with particular weaknesses that necessitate that we rely upon others in certain situations. Here, too, is humility at work.

Regardless, it is important to know how to cope when the battle feels too uphill. Here are a few tried-and-true suggestions.

Take preventive medicine. Before reaching wit's end, it is always good to have tools to help you avoid going down that road. Humor works wonders. So does having a sense of order and a schedule to work with. Everyone is different, so what works for you might not work for your sister-in-law and vice versa. And what worked last week might not work this week. Knowing yourself and your own weaknesses and trying to avoid setting yourself up for failure mitigates a lot of turmoil.

Keeping a healthy perspective on what constitutes a crisis can also help—there is nothing like having your perspective warped by lack of sleep, hormones, or teenagers (or all of the above). When a struggle seems to be consuming you, finding a diversion, such as calling a friend, going for a walk, or reading something totally unrelated to the topic of children, can go a long way.

Be kind to yourself. One of the struggles of motherhood is not simply the demands outside yourself, but the keen awareness of your own weaknesses. It is discouraging to watch yourself fall, yet again, into the same sins you thought you were gaining control over. St. Francis de Sales wisely advised women to be gentle in reproaching themselves; even our bitter reaction can be an indication of our own pride reeling from our failure to make ourselves perfect. The perfection can come only in the radical abandonment of ourselves to God. A gentle acceptance of our weaknesses (of which he is perfectly aware) can go much further than continued frustration and anger. Give yourself a lot of slack, especially when you know keenly the kind of stress you are managing.

Don't be afraid of tears. Tears are another one of those realities that just seem so cliché for women, but they are not without purpose. Interestingly, one Desert Father recommended tears to monks as a way to combat all sorts of spiritual ailments, such as discouragement. "The little child weeps when he is discouraged, when he needs help, when he needs to be loved. The same goes for adults who, somewhere deep down remain children. To weep is to acknowledge that one needs to be saved."[68]

Scientists have recently studied the content of tears—both those from cutting onions and those from our emotions. The emotional tears in the study contained hormones produced when the body is under stress. Tears are most likely a way to expel stress hormones from the body, which explains why a good cry can often leave us feeling better.[69] The tears from cutting onions had a much less complex biochemical profile.

While in some ways tears can feel like defeat—particularly when they show up without an invitation—they have a way of freeing us to move beyond our present struggles.

Make time to pray. Prayer and work—*ora et labora*. It is a teaching of the Church as old as the hills. As a mom, of course, you are working, but are you praying? Don't box yourself into thinking that prayer has to be formal—a set-aside time that will just add one more thing to your already busy schedule. Instead, let it be like quiet water that fills in the cracks of your day. If you are waiting to pick someone up, put your phone down and say a decade or two of the Rosary. If you hear an ambulance, say a Hail Mary. When you are struggling, be mindful that God is with you. There are countless little ways to let your mind and heart reach out to God throughout the day.

For mothers who are home most of the day, the monotony can be spirit crushing. We may be home, but there are so many distractions that our soul isn't really *at home*; that is to say, it isn't peaceful, joyful, gracious, and gentle. Finding ways to continually lift our hearts up to God throughout the day brings the right balance to our souls and opens us up to really hearing what the Lord is whispering back to us. "Sometimes," a priest friend once told me, "Jesus wants to share something personal about himself with you." Are we listening? Moms are used to listening with attentive ears to the needs and prattle of their children; the same skill is needed when listening for the quiet voice of Christ. We discussed previously how it is truly a part of the feminine vocation for God to speak to our hearts.

The offering of our pains and sacrifices back to God is an additional type of prayer. Giving him struggles, irritations, heartbreak—large or small—is essential in the effort to forget ourselves while allowing growth in love for him. He accepts even our failures. He can transform all of these into the unimaginable, if we let him.

Remember the saints. The saints, souls in purgatory, and our guardian angels are with us and are anxious to help us if we ask. A dear friend of mine, Nora, died six years ago. She was a Montessori teacher, so I often invoke her help when trying to make decisions about educating my children. One day I was missing her so much that I said, "Could you please just send me some roses so I know you are with me and helping me? I just miss you." Within a week, my husband returned from a trip to Walmart with a dozen white roses. I asked him why. His response: "Oh, just because." But he is not a just-because kind of guy and he hasn't done it since. Not only did I love the flowers, I knew Nora had sent him on this errand.

Often it seems like the world is falling apart around us. Our home can be a sanctuary of love, sanity, and order. The family Rosary is vital—even if the experience is less than rosy with little ones, do it anyway. The fruit will amaze you. The book *The Little Oratory* has great thoughts on how to help make your home truly a peaceful shelter from the cultural storm.[70]

Find like-minded moms. I noticed on a field trip what a dramatic a difference there is between having one or two children compared with four. I found the experience draining—mostly, I realized later, because my family's lifestyle is so different. Generally I think of this as a good thing, but sometimes being the odd man out and having your struggles underscored can be deflating. It is important to be around people who will affirm the decisions you have made to be open to the blessing of many children, even if it is only occasionally. Swimming upstream is normal in a culture like ours, but everyone needs a rest now and again. These women don't have to be your best friends, but people you can trust and relax with as you face the cultural battles together.

Don't forget friends without children. One never knows from where help may come. I've been blessed by three remarkable women who are indispensable. Unable to have biological children, these women have repeatedly stepped in during daily struggles, lightening the load with their attention, humor, a shared glass of wine, and conversations that go beyond mommyhood. When I was ordered to stay off my feet while pregnant, two of them came to my house and rearranged all the nursery items I hadn't been able to organize before the baby's arrival. And the three of them took shifts with my family and brought and cooked meals when junior finally arrived. The gift of their lives has led me to understand the importance of spiritual motherhood, while also making me very aware of the gratitude I have for the gift of fertility.

I have also had the great blessing of being in close contact with spiritual mothers: nuns. I have come to think of these professional prayers as the mothers who mother moms. Their prayers and wisdom have a way of keeping one's spirit afloat when sending out an SOS. It is easy enough to reach out to them via phone or e-mail to ask them to pray for you or to request other special intentions.

Rely on Jesus—and on his mother. As Catholics, sometimes we forget to rely upon Christ. What makes our faith so compelling is that it has God, the Trinity of persons, at its heart and not some esoteric ideology. When we are suffering, we don't have to do mental gymnastics to try to ignore the pain, but we know that it, too, has value when united to Christ. Christ is present to us always, and we call upon him to be the balm of our souls and to both console and purify us through whatever is going on in our lives. And unlike any other religion, Christianity is not man's search for God, but God's search for us. He is already waiting for you—you need not go looking for him.

Anytime Christ is made present, it is through the Holy Spirit and Mary. While the other saints are fantastic to have on your side, Mary is the patroness par excellence because she is always the Christ bearer. She understands every sorrow, struggle, and failure, and with the heart of a mother, she is with us in every triumph and tragedy.

Sometimes it can be difficult to relate to Mary; Scripture says little about her and she was sinless, after all. How can the rest of us relate to someone conceived without sin? Often it can be easier to get a better idea of something through comparison. We know that she is a perfect mother—so what do we as real mothers do, even in our sinfulness? We are the anchors of our family. There is no more real way to understand this than when you see the devastation when a mother dies, leaving behind a husband and small children. In her absence, nothing is the same at home. Mary, of course, is our spiritual mother and more devoted, loving, sacrificing, approachable, and insightful than any woman we can possibly imagine. Blessed Mary of Agreda, a sixteenth-century nun who received the special gift of the details of Mary's life, wrote about how much Mary desires that we let her love us. "Thou wilt have in Her a Mother to love thee, a Friend to counsel thee, a Mistress to direct thee, a Protectress to shield thee and a Queen whom thou canst serve and obey as handmaid."[71] What more could we need?

Questions for Reflection

1. What struggles have you faced in the past, and how did you get through them?

2. What are some ways you can think of to let off steam or preempt a bad situation?

3. In what ways can you rely more upon Christ, Mary, and the saints during times of struggle?

TWELVE

The Spark of Divine Love

Without love, deeds, even the most
brilliant, count as nothing.

—St. Thérèse of Lisieux[72]

One October, while at the pumpkin patch with my daughter's school, I found myself chatting with some other moms. I mentioned that I planned to start homeschooling after kindergarten. "So when are you going to get your life back?" was the sharp response of one mom. My mind reeled. How could I respond with a pithy answer? How could I explain to this woman that I didn't need *my* life back? How could I make her understand that, after all the years of living as a single woman and traveling the world, the personal fulfillment my children gave me was beyond everything I'd done up to that point? That when I had a "life" I was terribly lonely and dreaded Sunday evenings more than anything—the lowest part of the week, when there was nothing I could do to distract myself from my own loneliness. And how could I explain that with the arrival of each child, my heart and my commitment to being their mom grew to the point of not caring much about *my* life anymore? There is no sound bite that captures these realities. There is simply no way to explain to someone who is thoroughly secular the idea of vocation and the peace and joy that come with living that out.

The world laments the powerlessness, the weakness, the hiddenness of women who stay home with their children. Couldn't they be doing a lot more good outside the home? The short answer is no.

Each one of us has a unique and particular call—something only we can do for God. All it requires is for us to say yes—to give our fiat like Mary did so many centuries ago. Often our vocation starts with a simple itch of interest and ends up becoming something beyond our wildest dreams. Women have lives with distinct seasons. What we can't do now, we may be able to do in the future and vice versa. Our understanding of our own vocation expands over time, but God leaves hints hidden in the depths of our hearts; we can see his fingerprints in the hymns and Scripture passages that move us, in the virtues of others to which we are drawn, the ministries that inspire us, the saints we would love to have met. There is a pattern to all of it, if only we have the eyes to see it. That is also where silence comes in to inform our hearts, to clear away the distractions and focus our minds again on that "still, small voice" (1 Kings 19:12).

While all of these things we have discussed may seem small and insignificant, quite the contrary is true. Our lives are like weaving tapestries—we only get to see one knot at time, or the messy frame of the moment, but never the side with the actual design on it. And yet, we know from the saints that small things done with great love can change the world. "[I]n the divine economy of salvation," says Stein, "no sincere effort remains fruitless even when human eyes can perceive nothing but failures."[73] Like the two fish and five loaves offered by the little boy, Christ can transform the little things into something that will feed five thousand.

My Life for Yours

Blessed Archbishop Romero described motherhood as a type of martyrdom. A mother "conceives a child in her womb, brings him to life, nurses him, helps him grow and attends to him with affection. It is to give one's life. It is martyrdom."[74] Interestingly, however, we all give our lives to something: hedonism, fighting aging, leisure, comfort—things that are not worth the dignity of our souls. There is something inherently beautiful about giving our lives for someone else.

Healthy cultures and civilizations all have one thing in common: a deep understanding (even if not always acted upon or articulated) that our lives have meaning because of the sacrifices we make for those who come after us, through loyalty to a clan, tribe, or wider society. This simple "our lives for theirs" approach is what has animated history for centuries. Think of the building of Notre-Dame Cathedral in Paris, which the early masons knew would never be finished in their lifetimes. "Our lives for theirs" is an easy barometer to see if a civilization is on the rise or in decline. When that order becomes inverted, like in ancient Rome or late-Renaissance Venice, where each man and woman lived just for himself, the civilization will decay and cease to exist.

The sexual revolution of the 1960s is a marked example of this inversion in the West with the arrival of the pill. Never in the history of the world had the fundamental link between human sexuality and reproduction been so decidedly unhinged, ushering in a new conception of sexuality. Sex became about many things: self-expression, self-gratification, exploration, desire, etc., but not about its main reason for existence: to propagate the species (while of course, as Catholics, we also recognize its importance for bonding a couple). The general "our life for theirs" attitude lived out by parents for centuries suddenly became suspect as self-gratification came into vogue. "Why would anyone voluntarily put themselves through all that hard work to raise a large family?" became the new model under which we live today.

And yet it is hard to imagine the spread of Christianity without women—think of St. Helen and her son Constantine and the conversion of the Roman Empire to Christianity, or St. Augustine without St. Monica. Women have played a critical role in shaping history, particularly by converting the hearts of their husbands and sons through their own holiness: St. Cecilia, St. Rita, St. Francesa of Rome, to name a few. The same hand that has rocked the cradle has changed the world, for good or for ill. We see the negative of this in our current world: As women have abandoned their role as mothers, their children, now adults, feel neglected, lonely, empty, and without the interior resources to bridge the gap between what they lack and what they need to fill it. Suffering from what some call the "mother wound," these children never got the undivided attention and unconditional love they still so deeply crave. Our motherhood is not just about you or your family; it reaches beyond anything you can imagine, for better or worse.

The Age of the Christian Mother

The past six decades have produced an abundance of work on Our Lady. Starting in the 1950s, and particularly during John Paul II's lengthy pontificate, the popes have written explicitly about Mary's central role in salvation history. There have been numerous claims of Marian apparitions around the world, and while the Church has not yet made a determination about most of them, the message over and over again is to pray the Rosary. St. John Bosco, prophesying about the future, offered the Rosary and the Brown Scapular of Mary as the only steady course through future turmoil. St. Maximilian Kolbe, before his martyrdom at Auschwitz during World War II, set up a theological center with the sole purpose of plumbing the depths of Mariology. This relatively recent surge of Mariology can give us the impression that the Church has always spoken of Mary so deeply and so passionately, but this is not the case. Of course, she has always been revered, but the pitch of her presence wasn't usually this high.

In 1974, a French priest, Fr. André Feuillet, published an interesting book, *Jesus and His Mother,* that I have already quoted here in several places. As the sexual revolution was gaining steam and the post-Vatican II chaos was at its peak, this wise theologian and Scripture scholar quietly published his work focused on the life of Mary and her proper place in salvation history. His conclusions in the book are quite startling:

> The Christian Church is presently experiencing a very severe crisis. The most evangelical way of viewing this, without in any way trying to minimize it and without ceasing to call evil what is so in fact, is to see in this terrible trial the *painful childbearing of a new Christian world.* Just like the time of the Passion of Christ, these times we live in are very especially the *Hour of the Woman.* Above all, therefore, the Hour of the Woman par excellence of the new covenant, the Hour of Mary.[75]

Fr. Feuillet explains that today's difficult times mimic in a spiritual way the pain and struggle of childbearing. And yet, like childbirth, the pain gives way to great joy; in this case, a new Christian world. Mary's role is critical because she is never absent from a trial, but always the Mother of the Church, present as she was at Calvary.

Fr. Feuillet continues, "One has the distinct impression that it is in the first place on Christian women, open and transparent as was the Virgin Mary to the breath of the Holy Spirit, that the solution to the present crisis depends."[76] It is Christian women, because of our distinct vocation, both our openness to interior stirrings of the Holy Spirit and our ability to give grace to others, who offer hope for the world. He continues: "The sacrificial offering of Mary, the generous 'yes' she pronounced—were these not the very starting points of our salvation?"[77] Christian women, because of our dependence on Mary and our role as mothers to the messianic people— the people of the Church—"govern" the renewal we await. He doesn't say "join in" or "participate in" this renewal. He uses much stronger language: Christian women *govern*, or rule over this renewal. He adds:

> They live at the very heart of the Church, the mystery of love which brings forth souls to a new life, and in these will restore to the Church that priesthood which it could never do without: men and women consecrated and proud of their consecration. Christian women can make their own the cry of St. Therese of the Child Jesus: "In the heart of the Church, my Mother, I will be love." By their generosity which impels them to offer themselves like Mary, by giving themselves over entirely to God in love, they reign over the Church in much the same way as Christian mothers worthy of the name are the queens as well as the heart of their home.[78]

Christian women, then, insofar as we live out our vocation, have an ability and call, as we saw in chapter three, not given to men: to bridge heaven and earth. "She is mediatrix of the incomparable divine joy which derives from the invisible presence and action of the Risen Christ, source of all spiritual resurrections, and thus the renewal we await."[79]

This renewal of divine love, Feuillet explains, "may strike us with the impact of a new revelation, but . . . in reality *will be no more than a return to the most pure sources of the Christian revelation*" [emphasis added].[80] It is the *ideas so old that they are new again* that will heal the wounded, cure the sick, lift the spirits of the despairing, and bring joy to the brokenhearted. It is this to which Christian women are called, if only we have the hearts to hear. We have the ability to reclaim our families, our communities, our world through small acts performed with great love. We are called to make divine love visible yet again.

Pope Francis has expressed his own admiration for the important vocation of mothers:

Mothers are an antidote to the spread of a certain self-centeredness, a decline in openness, generosity and concern for others. In this sense, motherhood is more than childbearing; it is a life choice, entailing sacrifice, respect for life, and commitment to passing on those human and religious values which are essential for a healthy society.[81]

Ultimately, the Argentine pope makes clear, "A society without mothers would be an inhuman society, because mothers are always able to witness, even in the worst moments, tenderness, dedication, moral strength."[82]

Ours is a beautiful calling, a beautiful vocation. The Lord beckons. Will we go out to meet him?

Questions for Reflection

1. How do you live out "my life for yours" in your daily life?

2. How can understanding the different seasons of a woman's life help to put the sacrifices of family in perspective?

3. Are there ways to be mindful of your important call as a Christian mother throughout the day, even when you're consumed by the mundane or belittled by the world?

Afterword

This book started out with a small idea: Motherhood is hard, but that hard can be good for us. I scratched the surface of this topic only to find something far deeper than I ever anticipated. I found, in a nutshell, ideas so old they are new again. These ideas, *so ancient and yet so new* (St. Augustine), are the fundamental call of every Christian woman in the role of motherhood—physical and spiritual. I have felt a bit like Bernadette Soubirous in the movie *The Song of Bernadette* when the future saint is told by the beautiful woman to dig in the dirt, and as she starts scratching, first a puddle of water appears, then more and more water, until there's an abundant spring, which still flows today. On the one hand, it is all very startling; on the other, it is what we should expect when we give our Lord little things to work with—he transforms them into something beautiful.

Being a woman today is a complicated reality with so many pressures, mixed messages, and the deep desires of our own hearts. The women of the Bible could scarcely believe their eyes when they had encounters with God, as we see with Mary: "How can this be, since I have no relations with a man?" (Luke 1:34). And yet these dark corners of incomprehension are where we are called to place our faith. Edith Stein, in her wisdom, wrote: "All our being and becoming and acting in time is ordered from eternity, has meaning for eternity, and only becomes clear to us if and insofar as we put it in the light of eternity."[83] As with the experiences of the holy women whom Christ loved, obscurity is brought to clarity through the light of faith.

So I will leave you with one last thought about the heights and depths of your call from St. Thérèse of Lisieux, even though you may be a mother slogging through the trials of daily life:

> It should be enough for me, Jesus, to be a Carmelite and, by union with You, the mother of souls. Yet I long for other vocations: I want to be a warrior, a priest, an apostle, a Doctor of the Church, a martyr. I should like to enlighten souls. I should like to wander the world, preaching Your Name. Nor should I be content to be a missionary for only a few years; I should like to be one till the end of time.
>
> These desires caused me a real martyrdom until I found chapters 12 to 13 of First Corinthians, and read that we cannot all be apostles, doctors, etc. I went on reading: "Be zealous for the better gifts. And I show unto you a yet more excellent way." Charity gave me the key to my vocation. I realized that love includes all vocations, is in all things, and because it is eternal, embraces every time and place.
>
> My vocation is love! It is You, Lord, who has given it to me. So in the heart of the Church I *will be love.*

You, Lord will descend to my nothingness and transform that nothingness into living fire.[84]

Burn on, dear mothers!

About the Author

Carrie Gress has a doctorate in philosophy from the Catholic University of America and was the Rome bureau chief of Zenit's English edition. She is the co-author with George Weigel of *City of Saints: A Pilgrimage to John Paul II's Krakow* and the author of *Nudging Conversions*, published by Beacon Publishing in 2015. A mother of four, she and her family live in Virginia.

Notes

1   Letter of Pope John Paul II to Women, June 29, 1995. https://w2.vatican.va/content/john-paul-ii/en/letters/1995/documents/hf_jp-ii_let_29061995_women.html.

2   Pope Francis address, January 7, 2015. https://zenit.org/articles/pope-s-general-audience-address-on-mother-church-and-motherhood/.

3   Edith Stein, *Woman: Collected Works*, Vol. 2, trans. Freda Mary Oben (Washington, DC: ICS Publications, 1996), 132–3.

4   David Daley, "Camille Paglia: How Bill Clinton Is like Bill Cosby," *Salon*, July 28, 2015, http://www.salon.com/2015/07/28/camille_paglia_how_bill_clinton_is_like_bill_cosby/.

5   Ibid.

6   Denise C. McAllister, "Hey Madonna, You're Doing Sexy Wrong," *The Federalist*, April 20, 2015, http://thefederalist.com/2015/04/20/hey-madonna-youre-doing-sexy-wrong/#.VTbKcgp5y0U.facebook.

7   André Feuillet, *Jesus and His Mother* (Still River, MA: St. Bede's Publications, 1973), 207.

8   Catherine Brown Tkacz, "Women and the Church in the New Millennium," *St. Vladimir's Theological Quarterly* 52, no. 3–4 (2008): 243–74.

9   Pope Paul VI, Gaudium et Spes: Pastoral Constitution on the Church in the Modern World (Vatican City: Libreria Editrice Vaticana, 1965), Paragraph 24.

10   Servais Pinckaers, *The Sources of Christian Ethics*, trans. Mary Thomas Noble (Washington, DC: The Catholic University of America Press, 1995), 30.

11   William O. Brady, "Rituale Romanum: Instruction on the Day of Marriage and Exhortation Before Marriage," Sancta Missa, http://www.sanctamissa.org/en/resources/books-1962/rituale-romanum/66-matrimony-instruction.html.

12   Frank Pittman, *Man Enough* (New York: Perigee Books, 1994), 274.

13   Feuillet, *Jesus and His Mother*, 220.

14   Edith Stein, *Woman: Collected Works*, Vol. 2, trans. Freda Mary Oben (Washington, DC: ICS Publications, 1996), 51.

15   Ibid., 45.

16   Ibid., 73.

17   Ibid., 45.

18   Ibid., 78.

19   Feuillet, *Jesus and His Mother*, 241.

20   Ibid., 220.

21   Stein, *Woman*, 45.

22   Feuillet, *Jesus and His Mother*, 198.

23   Ibid., 240–1.

24   Stein, *Woman*, 101.

25   Ibid., 56.

26   Ibid., 48.

27   Ibid.

28   Ibid., 109.

29   W. Bradford Wilcox, "Moms Who Cut Back at Work Are Happier," *Atlantic*, December 18, 2013, http://www.theatlantic.com/business/archive/2013/12/moms-who-cut-back-at-work-are-happier/282460/.

30   Stein, *Woman*, 54.

31   Helen Andelin, *Fascinating Womanhood* (New York: Bantham Books, 1990).

32   Meg Meeker, *Strong Fathers, Strong Daughters* (New York: Ballantine Books, 2007).

33   Junno Arocho Esteves, "Pope's Morning Homily: Mothers and Grandmothers Are First in Transmitting Faith, *Zenit,* January 26, 2015, http://zenit.org/articles/pope-s-morning-homily-mothers-and-grandmothers-are-first-in-transmitting-faith/.

34   Zenit Staff, "Pope's General Audience Address: On Mother Church and Motherhood," *Zenit,* January 7, 2015, http://www.zenit.org/en/articles/pope-s-general-audience-address-on-mother-church-and-motherhood.

35   Feuillet, *Jesus and His Mother,* 196.

36   Ibid.

37   Lewis Alexander Leonard, *Life of Charles Carroll of Carrollton* (Charleston, SC: BiblioLife, 2014), online reprint of 1918 original, 8.

38   For more on the history of virtues and Christian moral ethics, see Servais Pinckaers, *The Sources of Christian Ethics.*

39   See Art and Laraine Bennett, *The Temperament God Gave You* (Manchester, NH: Sophia Institute Press, 2005) for further information about the classical temperaments.

40   Jorge Mario Bergoglio, *The Way of Humility* (San Francisco: Ignatius Press, 2014), 81–2.

41   Stein, *Woman,* 73.

42   Thomas McDermott, OP, *Catherine of Siena: Spiritual Development in Her Life and Teaching* (Mahwah, NJ: Paulist Press, 2008), 29.

43   Stein, *Woman,* 46–7.

44   "Quotes for Isobel Crawley," IMDb, http://www.imdb.com/character/ch0265541/quotes.

45   Aaron Green, "'La donna e mobile' Text and Translation," About.com, http://classicalmusic.about.com/od/opera/qt/ladonnaemobile.htm.

46   Zenit Staff, "Pope's General Audience Address."

47   Ibid.

48   "Oration 41," New Advent, http://www.newadvent.org/fathers/310241.htm.

49   Stein, *Woman*, 110.

50   Ibid., 46–7.

51   Ibid., 110.

52   Jean-Charles Nault, O.S.B., *The Noonday Devil: Acedia, the Unnamed Evil of Our Times* (San Francisco, Ignatius Press, 2015), 43.

53   http://www.forbes.com/sites/geoffloftus/2012/05/09/if-youre-going-through-hell-keep-going-winston-churchill/#21e7db273a3b

54   St. Catherine of Siena, *Saint Catherine of Siena as Seen in Her Letters*, trans. Vida A. Scudder (New York: J. M. Dent and Co., 1905), 37.

55   For more on St. Ignatius of Loyola's principles of discernment, see Timothy M. Gallagher, *The Discernment of Spirits* (New York: Crossroads Publishing, 2005).

56   Stein, *Woman*, 97.

57   Ibid.

58   Fr. Thomas Morrow, in his book *Overcoming Sinful Anger* (Manchester, NH: Sophia Institute Press, 2015), discusses how anger, more than any other emotion, is at the heart of divorce.

59   Stein, *Woman*, 102–3.

60   "Saintly Quotes," Catholic Tradition, http://www.catholictradition.org/Saints/saintly-quotes30.htm.

61   "Prayer of Saint Teresa of Avila," EWTN, https://www.ewtn.com/Devotionals/prayers/StTeresaofAvila.htm.

62   St. Thomas Aquinas, *Summa Theologica*, Vol. 3 (New York: Cosimo, 2013), 1377.

63   Stein, *Woman*, 132–3.

64   Pope John Paul II, *Mulieris Dignitatem* (Boston: St. Paul Books and Media, 1988), #27

65   Stein, *Woman*, 126.

66   Pope John Paul II, *Mulieris Dignitatem*, #27.

67   AZ Quotes, http://www.azquotes.com/quote/758769.

68   Nault, *The Noonday Devil*, 37.

69   Anton Skorucak, "The Science of Tears," ScienceIQ.com, http://www.scienceiq.com/facts/scienceoftears.cfm.

70   David Clayton and Leila Marie Lawler, *The Little Oratory* (Manchester, NH: Sophia Institute Press, 2014).

71   Mary of Agreda, *The Mystical City of God*, trans. Fiscar Marison (Charlotte, NC: Tan Books), 127.

72   "Thérèse de Lisieux > Quotes," Good Reads, http://www.goodreads.com/author/quotes/248952.Th_r_se_de_Lisieux.

73   Stein, *Woman*, 107.

74   Zenit Staff, "Pope's General Audience Address."

75   Feuillet, *Jesus and His Mother*, 239.

76   Ibid., 241.

77   Ibid.

78   Ibid.

79   Ibid.

80   Ibid.

81   Zenit Staff, "Pope's General Audience Address."

82   Ibid.

83   Stein, *Woman*, 88.

84   St. Thérèse of Lisieux, *Mornings with Saint Thérèse*, ed. Patricia Treece (Manchester, NH: Sophia Institute Press, 2015), 90–1.

Blessed

THE DYNAMIC CATHOLIC FIRST COMMUNION
&
FIRST RECONCILIATION EXPERIENCE

There's never been anything like this for children:
World-class animation. Workbooks with 250 hand-painted
works of art. Catechist-friendly leader guides, and incredible
content. Blessed isn't just different, it's groundbreaking.

**Request your FREE First Communion Program Pack &
First Reconciliation Program Pack
at *DynamicCatholic.com/BlessedPack***

EACH PROGRAM PACK INCLUDES:

- 1 DVD SET (42 ANIMATED SHORT FILMS)
- 1 STUDENT WORKBOOK
- 1 LEADER GUIDE
- 1 CHILDREN'S PRAYER PROCESS CARD

Just pay shipping.

Dynamic Catholic
Be Bold. Be Catholic.®

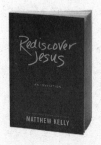

HAVE YOU EVER WONDERED HOW THE CATHOLIC FAITH COULD HELP YOU LIVE BETTER?

How it could help you find more *joy* at work, *manage* your personal finances, *improve* your marriage, or make you a *better* parent?

THERE IS GENIUS IN CATHOLICISM.

When *Catholicism* is lived as it is intended to be, it elevates every part of our lives. It may sound simple, but they say *genius is taking something complex and making it simple.*

Dynamic Catholic started with a dream: to help ordinary people discover the *genius of Catholicism.*

Wherever you are in your journey, we want to meet you there and walk with you, *step by step*, helping you to discover God and become *the-best-version-of-yourself.*

To find more helpful resources, visit us online at DynamicCatholic.com.

Dynamic Catholic

FEED YOUR SOUL.